Magnetic Love:

*The Last Book You'll Ever Need
to
Approach, Seduce, and Win Over
the Man or Men You Desire
by
Mastering the Art of Attraction
for Dating, Relationships,
and Marriage*

Sophia Newman

"Confidence is the spark, authenticity is the flame, and understanding is the fire that keeps desire burning. Master these, and the love you seek will come naturally."

~ Anonymous

.

"You don't attract what you want.
You attract what you are."

~ Dr. Wayne Dyer

Disclaimer

The information provided in this book is intended for educational and informational purposes only. It is not a substitute for professional advice, counseling, or therapy. The author and publisher are not licensed relationship counselors, therapists, or psychologists, and any advice provided should be used at your own discretion.

While the strategies and techniques presented in this book are based on research, personal experiences, and observations, individual results may vary. Relationships and human interactions are complex, and no single method or approach can guarantee success in every situation. It is important to approach dating and relationships with honesty, respect, and a commitment to mutual consent and understanding.

The content in this book is meant to empower readers to improve their confidence and interpersonal skills. It is not intended to encourage manipulation, deceit, or unethical behavior. The author and publisher do not condone any actions that violate another person's boundaries, autonomy, or well-being. Readers should also be aware that societal and cultural norms regarding dating and relationships may vary, and some advice may not be applicable or relevant in all contexts or cultures. It is the responsibility of the reader to adapt the information to their specific circumstances and values.

The author and publisher shall not be held liable for any damages, loss, or outcomes resulting from the use or misuse of the information contained in this book. By reading this book, you acknowledge and agree that you are solely responsible for your actions and decisions in any personal or romantic interactions.

If you require professional guidance for emotional, psychological, or relational challenges, we strongly encourage you to seek the assistance of a licensed therapist, counselor, or relationship expert.

Note to the Reader

As you read through this book, it's important to acknowledge the role technology has played in its creation. AI tools were used to assist with researching, formatting, organizing, and editing the material presented here. These tools helped ensure that the content is thorough, well-structured, and easy to follow. By combining technology with insights into human relationships and psychology, this book aims to offer you practical and effective advice that's rooted in both experience and accessible knowledge.

While AI played a significant role in streamlining the writing process, every idea, strategy, and recommendation in this book was curated with care and intentionality. The goal was always to provide you with valuable, actionable information that empowers you in your dating and relationship endeavors. It's worth noting that, while AI tools are incredibly useful in organizing and processing information, the heart of this book comes from understanding real-life dynamics and the desire to help others achieve personal growth. Relationships are deeply human, and this guide is ultimately about connecting authentically with yourself and the people you desire.

Thank you for trusting this book to be a part of your journey. I hope it provides you with the tools and inspiration you need to create the love life you deserve.

Magnetic Love:

*The Last Book You'll Ever Need
to Approach, Seduce, and Win Over
the Man or Men You Desire by
Mastering the Art of Attraction
for Dating, Relationships,
and Marriage*

Table of Contents

Introduction

In a world filled with dating apps, hookup culture, and complicated relationships, mastering the art of attraction might feel more overwhelming than ever. Whether you're looking to casually date, find a committed relationship, or even settle down in marriage, there's one universal truth: women have the power to attract and choose the men they desire. The key lies in understanding how to unlock that power and use it confidently.

This book isn't just another shallow guide about "getting the guy" or "playing games." Instead, it's designed to give you actionable tools and strategies to approach, seduce, and connect with men on a deeper level. This isn't just about surface-level attraction—this is about mastering yourself first, so you naturally attract the men who align with your goals and desires.

Think about it: attraction starts with you. Confidence, self-awareness, and authenticity are magnetic. When you understand how to approach a man with ease, flirt with intention, and spark undeniable chemistry, the entire dynamic changes. Men will feel drawn to you—not because of tricks, but because of the energy you project.

But what happens after you've caught his attention? Seduction is about more than just physical allure. It's about emotional connection, creating intrigue, and being the kind of woman he can't stop thinking about. You'll learn how to communicate in ways that captivate him, foster deeper intimacy, and keep him invested in you emotionally and physically.

This guide is comprehensive—it covers every step of the journey. From mastering first impressions to sustaining passion in a long-term relationship, you'll discover actionable advice tailored to every stage of the process. And, most importantly, you'll learn how to approach dating and relationships with a mindset rooted in confidence, self-respect, and clarity about what you want.

But why is this *the last book you'll ever need*? Because the strategies in this book are timeless. They're rooted in human nature, psychology, and understanding what truly makes men tick. Once you understand these principles, you'll never feel lost or powerless in your interactions with men again.

Here's what you'll gain:

- The confidence to approach any man, whether in-person or online, without fear or anxiety.

- Tools to create powerful first impressions and spark instant chemistry.

- Techniques to build emotional intimacy and connection while keeping the passion alive.

- A deeper understanding of male psychology—what they desire, what they fear, and what they need to commit.

- A roadmap to navigate modern dating challenges and avoid common pitfalls.

This isn't just about finding any man—it's about finding *the* man who aligns with your desires, respects your boundaries, and treats you the way you deserve. Whether you're looking to casually date, start a relationship, or build a future with someone special, this book will equip you with everything you need.

Get ready to transform the way you approach men and relationships. Once you unlock these strategies, the power will be in your hands. The possibilities are endless, and the life you desire is closer than you think.

Let's dive in—you're about to become an unstoppable force of attraction, seduction, and confidence. This is the last book you'll ever need.

Chapter 1: Understanding What Men Want: The Psychology of Attraction

The foundation of successful dating, seduction, and long-term relationships begins with one crucial understanding: what men truly want. While it's easy to fall into the trap of thinking that men are simple or only driven by surface-level desires, the truth is far more nuanced. Attraction is a complex interplay of biology, psychology, and social dynamics. By understanding these elements, you can position yourself as a woman who effortlessly captures the attention and interest of the men you desire.

In this chapter, we'll delve into the psychology of attraction, uncovering the traits, behaviors, and qualities that men universally find appealing. But this isn't about changing who you are—it's about harnessing your authentic self in ways that align with male psychology and human connection.

1.1 The Science of Attraction

Attraction is both instinctual and subjective. On a biological level, men are often wired to seek partners who display signs of health, vitality, and fertility. These traits, deeply rooted in evolution, explain why certain physical and behavioral cues—like confidence, a genuine smile, and warmth—can ignite instant interest. However, modern attraction goes beyond biology. Social and cultural factors play a significant role in shaping what men desire.

Key biological triggers for men include:

- **Physical Signals of Health:** Clear skin, good posture, and a vibrant appearance signal vitality.

- **Femininity:** Traits like softness, warmth, and nurturing tendencies often complement masculine energy.

- **Facial Expressions and Smiling:** A genuine smile is a universal symbol of approachability and positivity.

But physical attraction is just the starting point. Once you've caught a man's eye, emotional and intellectual compatibility become the driving factors. Men desire women who intrigue them, challenge them, and bring positivity to their lives.

1.2 The Three Pillars of Male Desire

To understand what men want, it's helpful to break it down into three main categories: emotional, intellectual, and physical desires.

1. Emotional Desire: Connection and Admiration

Men, like women, crave emotional intimacy. They want to feel understood, appreciated, and admired. While society often portrays men as emotionally detached, they are deeply affected by their emotional environment. A woman who can create a space where he feels safe and validated is someone he won't want to let go.

- **Be Supportive:** Men are drawn to women who can encourage them without judgment. Whether it's listening to his dreams or cheering him on during challenges, emotional support is vital.

- **Show Appreciation:** Compliments, gratitude, and recognition of his efforts make him feel valued.

- **Create Comfort:** Men appreciate partners who can bring a sense of calm and warmth to their lives, especially in a world that often demands them to "man up" and suppress vulnerability.

2. Intellectual Desire: Stimulating His Mind

While physical attraction may spark initial interest, intellectual connection keeps it alive. Men want to engage with women who challenge their thinking, share similar values, and bring something new to the table.

- **Be Curious:** Showing interest in his hobbies, work, or passions demonstrates your willingness to connect on a deeper level.

- **Express Your Opinions:** Men respect women who are confident in their perspectives and aren't afraid to share them.

- **Keep Learning:** A curious and growth-oriented mindset is magnetic. When you're constantly evolving, you remain exciting and intriguing.

3. Physical Desire: Attraction and Chemistry

Let's not shy away from the fact that physical attraction matters. Men are visual creatures, and a confident, well-presented woman naturally draws their attention. However, physical attraction isn't just about appearance—it's about how you carry yourself.

- **Confidence is Key:** Nothing is more attractive than a woman who is comfortable in her own skin.

- **Body Language:** Open, relaxed body language signals approachability and warmth. Maintaining eye contact, using light touches, and standing tall can make a significant impact.

- **Effort Matters:** Taking care of your appearance—not for him, but for yourself—projects self-respect and pride in who you are.

1.3 Common Myths About What Men Want

There's no shortage of misconceptions when it comes to what men desire. These myths often lead women down unproductive paths, creating frustration and confusion. Let's debunk some of the most common ones:

Myth #1: Men Only Care About Looks

While physical attraction is important, it's far from the only factor. In fact, many men prioritize emotional compatibility and shared values over superficial traits. A man may initially notice your appearance, but it's your personality and energy that keep him coming back.

Myth #2: Men Fear Commitment

Not all men are afraid of settling down. The key is understanding that men are more likely to commit when they feel emotionally secure and valued in the relationship. It's not about avoiding commitment—it's about finding the right person to commit to.

Myth #3: You Need to Play Games to Keep Him Interested

One of the most damaging myths is the idea that manipulation or "playing hard to get" is necessary to maintain a man's interest. While maintaining a sense of mystery can be intriguing, genuine connections are built on authenticity, not games.

1.4 Self-Awareness: The True Key to Attraction

Now that we've explored what men want, it's time to turn the lens inward. The most attractive women aren't those who try to mold themselves into someone else's ideal—they're the ones who know and love themselves deeply. Self-awareness is the foundation of magnetism.

Steps to Build Self-Awareness:

- **Identify Your Strengths:** What makes you unique? Celebrate those qualities and let them shine.

- **Embrace Vulnerability:** It's okay to have flaws and insecurities. Showing vulnerability makes you relatable and human.

- **Set Boundaries:** Knowing your worth means refusing to settle for less than you deserve. Strong boundaries communicate self-respect.

- **Focus on Growth:** Confidence stems from continuously working to improve yourself—physically, emotionally, and intellectually.

When you prioritize your own growth and happiness, you naturally become more attractive to others. Men are drawn to women who radiate self-assuredness, passion, and joy.

1.5 Practical Exercise: Shifting Your Focus

To apply the principles of this chapter, take some time to reflect on the following:

1. **Write Down Your Best Traits:** List at least five qualities you love about yourself. These could be physical, emotional, or intellectual. Focus on what makes you uniquely attractive.

2. **Identify What You Want in a Man:** What qualities are non-negotiable for you? Understanding what you desire will help you attract men who align with your goals.

3. **Practice Positive Self-Talk:** Replace negative thoughts about yourself with affirmations that highlight your strengths. For example, instead of "I'm not attractive enough," try "I radiate confidence and beauty in my own way."

Conclusion

Understanding what men want begins with understanding yourself. Attraction is not about pretending to be someone you're not; it's about amplifying the best parts of who you already are. By recognizing the emotional, intellectual, and physical desires that drive men, you can approach relationships with clarity and confidence.

In the next chapter, we'll dive deeper into building unshakable confidence— the foundation of your power in attraction, seduction, and lasting connection. Remember, everything starts with you. Let's unlock that potential together.

Chapter 2: Building Unshakable Confidence: The Foundation of Your Power

Confidence is the key that unlocks every door in life—whether it's approaching a man you're interested in, commanding attention in a room, or maintaining a healthy relationship. It's the foundation of attraction, the trait that amplifies all others, and the quality that makes people gravitate toward you effortlessly. Without confidence, even the most beautiful or accomplished woman can feel invisible. But with confidence, you become unstoppable.

The good news? Confidence isn't something you're born with—it's a skill you can build. In this chapter, we'll explore why confidence is essential, how to develop it, and practical strategies to radiate self-assuredness in every area of your life.

2.1 Why Confidence is So Magnetic

Think about the people you admire most. Chances are, it's not just their looks or accomplishments that make them stand out—it's their energy. Confidence is magnetic because it signals to others that you value yourself and are comfortable in your own skin.

Here's why confidence is so attractive to men:

- **It Signals Self-Worth:** Confidence communicates that you know your value and won't settle for less. This self-assuredness is irresistible.

- **It Radiates Positivity:** Confident people exude an energy that draws others in. They're fun to be around because they uplift and inspire.

- **It Reduces Neediness:** When you're confident, you're not looking for a man to complete you or validate you. This independence is highly appealing.

Men are naturally drawn to women who carry themselves with self-respect and poise. A confident woman doesn't need to prove her worth; she simply knows it.

2.2 The Confidence Myth

Many people mistakenly believe that confidence is tied to external factors like appearance, success, or social status. While these things can contribute, true confidence comes from within. It's about how you perceive yourself—not how others perceive you.

This means you don't need to be a supermodel, have a six-figure salary, or have an Instagram-worthy life to be confident. You simply need to embrace who you are and own it.

2.3 The Three Pillars of Confidence

To build unshakable confidence, focus on three key areas:

1. Self-Awareness: Know Yourself

Confidence starts with understanding and accepting who you are. This includes your strengths, values, and even your imperfections.

How to Build Self-Awareness:

- **Reflect on Your Strengths:** Write down what you're good at—whether it's your sense of humor, your kindness, or your creativity.

- **Identify Your Values:** What matters most to you in life and relationships? Knowing your values helps you stand firm in your choices.

- **Embrace Your Flaws:** Nobody is perfect, and that's okay. Your imperfections make you human and relatable.

2. Self-Care: Value Yourself

Taking care of yourself physically, emotionally, and mentally is a powerful way to boost confidence. When you treat yourself with love and respect, it shows.

How to Practice Self-Care:

- **Focus on Health:** Eat well, exercise, and get enough sleep. A healthy body fuels a confident mind.

- **Grooming and Style:** Wear clothes that make you feel good and take pride in your appearance—not for others, but for yourself.

- **Set Boundaries:** Don't let others take advantage of you. Learn to say no to things that drain your energy or don't align with your values.

3. Mindset: Believe in Yourself

Your mindset is everything. The way you think about yourself and the world directly impacts your confidence.

How to Cultivate a Confident Mindset:

- **Challenge Negative Thoughts:** Replace self-doubt with empowering beliefs. For example, instead of "I'll never attract someone like him," tell yourself, "I'm a catch, and the right man will see that."

- **Visualize Success:** Picture yourself confidently approaching someone, excelling in a conversation, or walking into a room with ease. Visualization can help make confidence a reality.

- **Practice Gratitude:** Focus on what's going well in your life instead of what's lacking. Gratitude shifts your perspective to positivity.

2.4 Practical Confidence-Building Exercises

Exercise 1: Power Posing

Your body language affects how you feel about yourself. Before a social event, date, or nerve-wracking situation, try this:

1. Stand tall with your shoulders back and your hands on your hips, like a superhero.

2. Hold this pose for two minutes while breathing deeply.

3. Notice how your mood and energy shift.

Exercise 2: The Compliment Journal

Every night, write down three things you like about yourself. They can be small (e.g., "I made someone laugh today") or big (e.g., "I aced that presentation"). Over time, this practice will help you focus on your positive qualities.

Exercise 3: Face Your Fears

Confidence grows when you step out of your comfort zone. Identify one thing you've been avoiding—whether it's striking up a conversation with a stranger or speaking up in a meeting—and challenge yourself to do it.

2.5 How Confidence Transforms Your Interactions with Men

When you exude confidence, your interactions with men naturally change:

- **You Become More Approachable:** A confident smile and open body language make men feel at ease.

- **You Command Respect:** Men are more likely to treat you with care and admiration when you carry yourself with self-assuredness.

- **You Attract the Right Men:** Confidence acts as a filter, repelling those who don't align with your values and drawing in those who do.

For example, imagine walking into a room knowing your worth. Instead of worrying about whether someone will notice you, you focus on enjoying yourself. This shift in mindset makes you magnetic, and men can't help but be intrigued by your energy.

2.6 The Confidence-Magnetism Loop

Confidence and attraction are part of a positive feedback loop. The more confident you are, the more positive attention you'll receive. This attention, in turn, boosts your confidence further. The key is to get the ball rolling by taking small steps toward self-assuredness every day.

Conclusion

Confidence is the foundation of everything you'll learn in this book. Without it, even the most effective seduction techniques will fall flat. But with it, you'll have the power to approach, connect with, and captivate the men you desire. Remember, confidence isn't about being perfect—it's about owning who you are and showing up as your authentic self.

In the next chapter, we'll take your newfound confidence and apply it to real-world scenarios. Get ready to learn how to make a stunning first impression and approach any man with ease.

Chapter 3: Mastering the First Impression: How to Approach Any Man with Ease

First impressions matter, especially when it comes to attraction. Within seconds of meeting someone, they form an opinion about you—based on your body language, appearance, energy, and how you present yourself. While this might sound intimidating, it's also empowering because it gives you an opportunity to make a conscious and memorable impact.

Approaching a man with confidence and grace is a skill that can open doors to meaningful connections. Whether you're at a bar, a coffee shop, a social event, or even on a dating app, knowing how to make a great first impression can set the tone for everything that follows.

In this chapter, we'll explore the art of creating a magnetic first impression, the steps to approach a man with ease, and practical techniques for breaking the ice and sparking genuine interest.

3.1 The Importance of First Impressions

Studies show that people form lasting impressions within the first 7 to 10 seconds of meeting someone. For men, this initial judgment is often based on:

1. **Body Language:** How you carry yourself communicates confidence, approachability, and warmth.

2. **Facial Expression:** A genuine smile can make you appear friendly and open.

3. **Energy:** Your vibe—positive, playful, or reserved—sets the tone for the interaction.

The good news? You don't need to be perfect to make a great first impression. You simply need to exude confidence and show that you're interested in connecting.

3.2 The Mindset Shift: Reframing Fear of Rejection

One of the biggest obstacles to approaching a man is fear of rejection. The thought of him not being interested can feel daunting, but rejection is rarely personal—it's often a reflection of timing, preferences, or circumstances.

Here's how to shift your mindset:

- **Focus on the Outcome You Can Control:** You can't control how someone responds, but you can control how you show up.

- **See Rejection as Redirection:** If he's not interested, it's a sign he wasn't the right match for you, and that's okay.

- **Celebrate Your Courage:** Every time you approach someone, you're building your confidence, regardless of the outcome.

The key is to approach interactions with curiosity rather than attachment to a specific result. Instead of thinking, *What if he doesn't like me?* ask yourself, *What can I learn from this interaction?*

3.3 Preparing to Approach: The Four Elements of a Great First Impression

Before you approach a man, there are a few key elements to consider:

1. Your Appearance

While attraction isn't solely about looks, how you present yourself matters. Dressing in a way that makes you feel confident and comfortable can boost your self-assurance and make you more approachable.

Tips:

- Wear clothes that fit well and flatter your body shape.
- Add a touch of color or a signature accessory to stand out.
- Prioritize good grooming—clean nails, styled hair, and fresh breath go a long way.

2. Your Body Language

Open and confident body language signals that you're approachable and interested.

Practice These Tips:

- Stand tall with your shoulders back.
- Make eye contact and smile warmly.
- Avoid crossing your arms or fidgeting, as these can signal nervousness or disinterest.

3. Your Energy

Your energy is what draws people in. A positive, lighthearted vibe is infectious and makes others want to be around you.

How to Radiate Positive Energy:

- Think about something that makes you genuinely happy before approaching someone.

- Keep your tone of voice upbeat and playful.

- Practice gratitude—it naturally enhances your mood and energy.

4. Your Intentions

Approach interactions with the goal of connection rather than impressing or "winning" someone over. When you're genuinely interested in the other person, it shows.

3.4 How to Approach a Man with Ease

Approaching a man can feel intimidating at first, but it doesn't have to be. By following these steps, you'll feel more confident and relaxed in any setting.

Step 1: Use Body Language to Signal Interest

Before walking up to him, use non-verbal cues to show you're open to interaction:

- **Make Eye Contact:** Hold his gaze for a couple of seconds, then look away with a small smile. This playful move signals interest.

- **Position Yourself Nearby:** Move closer to him casually so it's easier to start a conversation.

Step 2: Start with a Simple Opening Line

An approach doesn't have to be dramatic or rehearsed—sometimes, the simplest lines are the most effective.

Examples of Easy Icebreakers:

- "Hi, I just wanted to say you have a great smile."

- "I couldn't help but notice your [book/drink/shirt]—what's the story behind it?"

- "I'm curious—what's the best thing you've tried here so far?"

The key is to keep it light, natural, and conversational.

Step 3: Compliment or Show Curiosity

People love to feel appreciated and interesting. Complimenting him or asking a thoughtful question about something unique to him can immediately create a connection.

Compliment Ideas:

- "You seem really confident. I like that."

- "That jacket looks amazing on you—where did you get it?"

Curiosity Prompts:

- "You seem like someone with an interesting story—what's something most people don't know about you?"

- "What's your go-to drink here? I need recommendations."

Step 4: Be Playful and Authentic

Flirting is less about what you say and more about how you say it. A playful tone, a mischievous smile, and a touch of humor can make all the difference.

3.5 What to Do If He Doesn't Respond Well

Not every approach will lead to a positive response, and that's okay. If he doesn't seem interested, handle the situation gracefully:

- **Stay Positive:** Smile, thank him for his time, and move on.

- **Don't Take It Personally:** Attraction is subjective, and his lack of interest doesn't reflect your worth.

- **Celebrate Your Courage:** Every approach builds your confidence and makes future interactions easier.

3.6 Practical Exercises for Practicing Approaches

Exercise 1: Start Small

Practice making small talk with strangers in low-pressure situations, like a barista, a cashier, or someone in line at a store. This helps you build confidence in initiating conversations.

Exercise 2: Practice in Front of a Mirror

Rehearse your body language, smile, and opening lines in front of a mirror. Notice how you carry yourself and make adjustments to appear relaxed and confident.

Exercise 3: Eye Contact Challenge

Spend a day practicing holding eye contact with people you interact with. Start with brief moments and gradually extend the duration to build your comfort level.

Conclusion

Approaching a man doesn't have to be intimidating or complicated. By focusing on your body language, energy, and authenticity, you can make a powerful first impression that leaves him wanting to know more. Remember, the goal isn't perfection—it's connection.

In the next chapter, we'll explore the art of flirting and creating magnetic chemistry, taking your interactions to the next level. Get ready to unlock the secrets of effortless seduction.

Chapter 4: Creating Magnetic Chemistry: The Art of Flirting Without Fear

Flirting is an art, and when done right, it can transform a simple interaction into a spark-filled connection. It's the playful, lighthearted language of attraction—a subtle dance that teases, intrigues, and leaves the other person wanting more. While confidence sets the foundation for attraction, flirting is the electricity that creates chemistry.

Many people overcomplicate flirting, thinking it requires the perfect line or a specific set of skills. The truth is, the most effective flirting is natural and spontaneous, driven by your unique personality. This chapter will teach you how to flirt effortlessly, read the signs of mutual interest, and create the kind of magnetic chemistry that turns heads and melts hearts.

4.1 What Is Flirting and Why Does It Work?

At its core, flirting is about showing interest in someone while maintaining an air of playfulness and mystery. It's a way to gauge mutual attraction without outright stating your intentions. When you flirt, you're signaling two things:

1. **You're confident and comfortable with yourself.**
2. **You're interested in them, but not desperate.**

Flirting works because it's engaging and fun. It releases tension, creates excitement, and builds a sense of intrigue. It also activates the reward centers of the brain, making the interaction feel enjoyable and memorable.

4.2 The Essentials of Flirting

1. Confidence

Flirting is rooted in self-assurance. When you flirt, you're putting yourself out there in a playful way, so confidence is key. Even if you feel nervous, remind yourself that flirting is just a conversation with a little extra sparkle—it's not life or death.

2. Playfulness

Flirting is supposed to be fun! Keep things lighthearted and don't take yourself too seriously. A witty comment or a playful tease can make the interaction more engaging.

3. Subtlety

Good flirting is subtle—it hints at attraction without being overly explicit. Think of it as leaving breadcrumbs of interest rather than serving the whole loaf at once.

4.3 The Five Types of Flirting

Not everyone flirts in the same way, and that's what makes it so exciting. By understanding the different styles of flirting, you can find the approach that feels most authentic to you:

1. Physical Flirting

This involves using touch and body language to communicate interest. For example, lightly brushing his arm when laughing or standing close enough to create intimacy.

2. Witty Flirting

Humor is a powerful tool in flirting. Playful banter, clever comebacks, and inside jokes can create an instant connection.

3. Compliment-Based Flirting

Compliments that feel genuine and specific—like noticing his unique sense of style or how he carries himself—can make him feel appreciated.

4. Mysterious Flirting

This involves being intriguing and slightly elusive. Dropping hints about your interests or plans without giving everything away keeps him curious.

5. Energetic Flirting

This style relies on high-energy interactions, like enthusiastic conversations, laughter, and positive vibes that make the moment unforgettable.

4.4 Body Language: The Unspoken Flirtation

Non-verbal communication is one of the most powerful tools in flirting. Your body language can convey interest, confidence, and playfulness without saying a word.

Key Body Language Tips for Flirting:

1. **Make Eye Contact:** Lock eyes for a few seconds, then look away with a smile. This creates intrigue and signals interest.

2. **Smile Genuinely:** A warm, genuine smile is inviting and disarming.

3. **Lean In:** Subtly leaning toward him during the conversation shows engagement and attraction.

4. **Mirroring:** Mimic his gestures and posture subtly to create a sense of connection.

5. **Light Touches:** A gentle touch on his arm or shoulder can break the physical barrier and increase intimacy.

4.5 How to Flirt Naturally: Practical Tips

Flirting doesn't have to feel forced or awkward. Here are some ways to flirt naturally and authentically:

1. Start with Eye Contact and a Smile

The simplest and most effective way to flirt is to meet his eyes, hold the gaze for a second or two, and smile. This small gesture conveys interest and invites him to engage with you.

2. Compliment Him

Men love compliments just as much as women do. Compliment something specific about him, like his style, sense of humor, or confidence. For example:

- "I like how you think outside the box—that's rare."

- "You've got great taste in [music/art/food]. Where did you pick that up?"

3. Use Playful Teasing

Teasing is a fun way to create rapport and build tension. For example:

- "So, do you always charm strangers like this, or is today special?"

- "Are you trying to impress me with that story? Because it's working."

The key is to keep the teasing lighthearted and never cross into mean-spirited territory.

4. Show Genuine Interest

Flirting isn't just about you talking—it's about making him feel seen and appreciated. Ask thoughtful questions and listen actively to his answers. For example:

- "What's something you're passionate about that most people don't know?"

- "What's been the highlight of your week so far?"

5. Use Humor

A shared laugh is one of the fastest ways to build chemistry. Don't be afraid to crack a joke or share a funny story—it makes the interaction more memorable.

4.6 Reading the Signs: Is He Flirting Back?

Flirting is a two-way street. To know if he's interested, look for these signs:

1. **He Mirrors Your Energy:** If he matches your tone, body language, or enthusiasm, he's likely engaged.

2. **He Finds Reasons to Touch You:** A light touch on your hand or shoulder is a strong sign of attraction.

3. **He Asks Questions About You:** If he's curious about your life, it shows he's invested in the conversation.

4. **He Maintains Eye Contact:** Sustained eye contact often signals genuine interest.

5. **He Smiles Frequently:** A warm, natural smile is a clear indicator that he's enjoying the interaction.

If you notice these signals, it's a good sign that he's interested and enjoying the flirtation.

4.7 Overcoming Flirting Fears

If you're nervous about flirting, remember that it's a skill that improves with practice. Start small and give yourself permission to make mistakes. Flirting should feel fun, not like a test.

Mindset Shifts to Reduce Anxiety:

- **Stop Overthinking:** Flirting isn't about perfection; it's about connection.

- **Stay Playful:** Focus on having fun rather than achieving a specific outcome.

- **Don't Take Rejection Personally:** If he doesn't respond, it's not a reflection of your worth—it's simply not a match.

4.8 Practical Flirting Exercises

Exercise 1: Practice Playful Compliments

The next time you're out, compliment someone casually. For example:

- "That jacket looks great on you—where'd you get it?"
  This will help you build confidence in initiating light, flirtatious conversations.

Exercise 2: The 3-Second Rule

When you see someone you'd like to approach, give yourself three seconds to act. Don't overthink—just smile, walk over, and start a conversation.

Exercise 3: Flirt with Strangers

Practice flirting in low-stakes environments, like with a barista or a store clerk. This helps you refine your technique without pressure.

Conclusion

Flirting is about creating a playful, engaging connection that leaves the other person intrigued and wanting more. By mastering the art of subtlety, humor, and body language, you can spark undeniable chemistry with any man you meet.

In the next chapter, we'll take things a step further by exploring how to turn interest into desire with a step-by-step seduction blueprint. Get ready to unlock the secrets of irresistible allure.

Chapter 5: The Seduction Blueprint: Turning Interest Into Desire

Flirting may ignite a spark, but seduction is what turns that spark into a roaring flame. Seduction is not about manipulation or deceit—it's about creating an environment of desire, intrigue, and emotional connection. It's a dance of attraction where both people feel excited, engaged, and eager to explore each other further.

This chapter lays out a step-by-step blueprint to help you move from casual interest to undeniable desire. You'll learn how to build tension, maintain mystery, and deepen the connection while staying authentic and true to yourself. Whether you're looking for a fun fling or laying the foundation for a serious relationship, these strategies will help you captivate the men you desire.

5.1 The Psychology of Desire

Desire is rooted in both emotional and physical attraction, but the key to creating lasting desire lies in building tension and anticipation. Humans are wired to want what feels just out of reach—when something feels both attainable and slightly elusive, it becomes irresistible.

Men, in particular, are drawn to women who create a balance between availability and mystery. They enjoy the thrill of the chase, but only when the reward feels worth pursuing. Understanding this dynamic is essential to mastering the art of seduction.

5.2 The Three Phases of Seduction

To successfully move from interest to desire, follow these three phases:

1. Attraction: Capturing His Attention

This is the initial stage where you establish your presence and spark his curiosity. At this point, your goal is to make him notice you and see you as someone intriguing.

Key Tactics for Building Attraction:

- **Look and Feel Your Best:** Confidence in your appearance radiates outward, drawing people in.

- **Engage in Lighthearted Banter:** Keep the conversation fun and easygoing.

- **Use Playful Body Language:** Make eye contact, smile often, and lightly touch his arm or shoulder to create a sense of connection.

2. Intrigue: Keeping Him Hooked

Once you've captured his attention, the next phase is to build intrigue. This is where you create a sense of mystery and leave him wanting more.

How to Build Intrigue:

- **Be a Little Elusive:** Don't reveal everything about yourself right away. Drop hints about your interests, hobbies, or experiences without going into full detail. For example, say, "I have the funniest story about my last trip," and leave it at that—he'll want to know more.

- **Balance Curiosity and Availability:** Be warm and engaging, but don't always be too accessible. Let him work to earn your time and attention.

- **Maintain Your Independence:** Men are drawn to women who have their own passions, goals, and social lives. Show him that your world doesn't revolve around him.

3. Connection: Turning Interest Into Desire

This is where emotional intimacy and physical chemistry deepen. In this phase, you focus on creating a bond that feels unique and special.

How to Build Connection:

- **Share Vulnerabilities:** When the time feels right, open up about your life, dreams, or challenges. This creates emotional intimacy and trust.

- **Show Appreciation:** Compliment him on qualities you genuinely admire—his humor, intelligence, or kindness.

- **Build Physical Tension:** Use subtle physical cues, like brushing against him or lightly placing your hand on his knee, to escalate the attraction naturally.

5.3 The Role of Mystery in Seduction

Mystery is one of the most powerful tools in seduction. When you're a little unpredictable or enigmatic, you become intriguing. This doesn't mean playing games or being dishonest—it's about keeping a sense of excitement and discovery alive.

Ways to Cultivate Mystery:

1. **Don't Overshare:** Resist the urge to tell him everything about yourself right away. Let him uncover you gradually.

2. **Be Unpredictable:** Keep him guessing by switching up your routines. For example, if you always text first, let him reach out to you occasionally.

3. **Maintain Boundaries:** Let him know that while you enjoy his company, you also value your own time and space.

5.4 The Art of Building Sexual Tension

Sexual tension is the invisible thread that makes your connection irresistible. It's that charged energy that leaves both of you wanting more. Building sexual tension requires subtlety, timing, and an understanding of body language.

Tips for Creating Sexual Tension:

- **Prolonged Eye Contact:** Hold his gaze a little longer than usual, and let your eyes convey your interest.

- **Slow Movements:** Deliberate, unhurried gestures—like brushing your hair back or leaning in slightly—can heighten the anticipation.

- **Tease and Pause:** Lean in as if you're about to touch or whisper something, then pull back slightly. This creates a push-pull dynamic that's thrilling.

- **Use Your Voice:** Speak in a softer, slower tone when the conversation becomes more intimate.

5.5 Recognizing and Responding to His Signals

Seduction is a two-way street. Pay attention to how he responds to your cues—this will help you gauge his interest and adjust your approach.

Signs He's Interested:

- He leans toward you during the conversation.
- He mirrors your body language and energy.

- He finds excuses to touch you, even lightly.
- He compliments you or finds ways to keep the conversation going.

If you notice these signals, it's a sign that he's feeling the chemistry and is receptive to your advances.

5.6 Mistakes to Avoid in Seduction

While seduction is about playfulness and connection, there are common pitfalls that can derail the process.

Avoid These Mistakes:

1. **Being Too Aggressive:** Seduction is about subtlety. Coming on too strong can feel overwhelming or insincere.

2. **Faking Interest:** Don't pretend to like something just to impress him—authenticity is far more attractive.

3. **Losing Yourself:** It's easy to get caught up in trying to please someone, but always stay true to your values and boundaries.

5.7 Practical Seduction Exercises

Exercise 1: Practice the Push-Pull Dynamic

The next time you're in a conversation with someone you're attracted to, try this:

1. **Push:** Playfully tease or challenge him. For example, "Are you always this charming, or is today special?"

2. **Pull:** Follow up with a warm smile or a compliment. For example, "Seriously though, I love your sense of humor."

Exercise 2: Build Eye Contact Confidence

Spend a day practicing holding eye contact with people you interact with. Gradually extend the length of time you maintain eye contact—it's a powerful way to convey interest.

Exercise 3: Be Playfully Mysterious

In your next conversation, leave out one interesting detail about a story or experience. For example, "I once got lost in Paris, and the way I found my way back was crazy—but that's a story for another time." Watch how intrigued he becomes.

Conclusion

Seduction is a blend of confidence, playfulness, and emotional connection. By following this blueprint, you can turn casual interest into undeniable desire while staying authentic and true to yourself. Remember, the goal isn't to manipulate or control—it's to create a dynamic where both of you feel excited and engaged.

In the next chapter, we'll explore how to deepen emotional intimacy and communicate in ways that captivate his heart and mind. You're well on your way to mastering the art of attraction!

Chapter 6: Communicating Like a Goddess: Conversations That Captivate

Communication is the bridge between attraction and connection. While first impressions and flirtation can spark interest, meaningful conversations are what keep the flame alive. Men are drawn to women who can engage them emotionally and intellectually, making them feel understood, intrigued, and valued.

In this chapter, we'll explore the secrets to captivating conversations that leave a lasting impression. You'll learn how to listen actively, speak confidently, and navigate deeper topics while still keeping things fun and lighthearted. Whether you're talking to a man for the first time or building intimacy with someone you're dating, mastering the art of communication will transform your interactions.

6.1 Why Communication Is Key in Attraction

Men, like anyone else, want to feel heard, appreciated, and understood. A great conversation creates a sense of connection and trust, setting the stage for emotional intimacy and attraction.

Here's why communication is so powerful:

- **It Builds Emotional Intimacy:** Sharing your thoughts, values, and feelings deepens the bond between you.

- **It Creates Intrigue:** Asking thoughtful questions and sharing unique insights keeps the conversation exciting.

- **It Shows Confidence:** Speaking with clarity and conviction signals self-assuredness, which is highly attractive.

6.2 The Elements of Captivating Communication

1. Active Listening

One of the most overlooked aspects of great communication is listening. When you truly pay attention to what someone is saying, it shows that you value their thoughts and feelings.

Tips for Active Listening:

- **Make Eye Contact:** Look at him while he's speaking to show you're engaged.

- **Nod or Respond Naturally:** Use small verbal cues like "I see," or "That's interesting" to show you're following along.

- **Avoid Interrupting:** Let him finish his thoughts before you respond.

2. Open-Ended Questions

The best conversations are like a game of ping-pong—both people have a chance to contribute and keep the flow going. Open-ended questions encourage deeper and more meaningful exchanges.

Examples of Open-Ended Questions:

- "What's something you're really passionate about?"

- "What's the most exciting thing that's happened to you recently?"

- "If you could live anywhere in the world, where would it be and why?"

3. Playful Banter

While meaningful topics are important, playful banter adds an element of fun and flirtation. It keeps the energy light and prevents the conversation from becoming too serious too quickly.

How to Add Playful Banter:

- Use light teasing: "Are you always this competitive, or am I just lucky today?"

- Be a little dramatic: "Wow, you like pineapple on pizza? I don't know if we can be friends anymore."

- Laugh at yourself: "I tried to cook last night, and let's just say I'm probably banned from using the oven for a while."

4. Vulnerability

Opening up about your experiences, dreams, or fears creates a sense of authenticity and emotional connection. Vulnerability is what turns a casual conversation into a meaningful one.

How to Be Vulnerable Without Oversharing:

- Share stories that reveal your personality or values: "One of the scariest things I've done was move to a new city alone, but it taught me so much about myself."

- Let him see your quirks: "I'll admit, I'm the kind of person who gets way too excited about organizing my bookshelf."

- Be honest about your feelings in the moment: "This has been such a fun night—I feel like I haven't laughed this much in ages."

6.3 Communicating Confidence Through Your Words

The way you speak can say as much about your confidence as the words you choose. Men are naturally drawn to women who express themselves clearly and authentically.

Tips for Speaking Confidently:

1. **Use a Warm Tone:** Speak with energy and enthusiasm, but avoid sounding rushed or anxious.

2. **Avoid Filler Words:** Replace "um," "like," or "you know" with pauses that give your words more weight.

3. **Own Your Opinions:** Express your thoughts unapologetically. For example, instead of saying, "This might sound silly, but..." simply state your opinion.

4. **Stay Positive:** Focus on uplifting topics rather than complaining or gossiping. Positivity is contagious and attractive.

6.4 Creating Emotional Intimacy Through Conversation

Emotional intimacy is the foundation of lasting attraction. When you connect with a man on a deeper level, it creates a bond that goes beyond physical chemistry.

How to Build Emotional Intimacy:

- **Ask About His Feelings:** Instead of focusing only on surface-level topics, explore how he feels about his experiences. For example, "What did you love most about that trip?"

- **Share Your Values:** Talk about what matters most to you, like family, personal growth, or adventures you want to pursue.

- **Express Gratitude:** Show appreciation for his insights, stories, or efforts. For example, "I really admire how passionate you are about your work—it's inspiring."

6.5 Flirting Through Conversation

Flirty conversations are all about striking the right balance between playful and sincere. Here's how to keep the chemistry alive during your chats:

Use Double Entendres:

These playful comments have a hint of humor and intrigue. For example:

- "You must be trouble—I can just tell."

- "Do you always make such a strong first impression?"

Mirror His Energy:

Match his tone and level of enthusiasm. If he's joking and lighthearted, play along. If he's opening up, reflect that by being equally genuine.

Drop Subtle Compliments:

Compliment him in a way that feels effortless. For example:

- "I love how passionate you are—it's really refreshing."

- "You're surprisingly good at this—do you have some kind of secret talent?"

6.6 Handling Difficult or Awkward Moments

Not every conversation will flow perfectly, and that's okay. Knowing how to handle awkward moments with grace shows emotional intelligence and confidence.

How to Handle Awkward Silences:

1. **Acknowledge It Playfully:** "Well, that was a dramatic pause. Where were we?"

2. **Change the Subject:** Transition to a new topic with a question. For example, "By the way, what's your favorite way to unwind after a busy week?"

How to Navigate Disagreements:

- **Stay Calm:** Don't let the conversation become heated—focus on understanding his perspective.

- **Agree to Disagree:** Say something like, "I can see where you're coming from, even if I feel differently. It's interesting to hear your take on it."

6.7 Practical Conversation Exercises

Exercise 1: Practice Active Listening

During your next conversation, challenge yourself to listen without interrupting. After the person finishes speaking, summarize what they said before responding. This shows you're fully engaged.

Exercise 2: The 3-Question Rule

Make it a goal to ask three thoughtful, open-ended questions in every conversation. This helps you stay curious and keep the dialogue flowing.

Exercise 3: Playful Compliments

Practice giving genuine, playful compliments to people you interact with daily. This helps you build the habit of being engaging and attentive.

Conclusion

Mastering the art of captivating communication is one of the most powerful skills you can develop in dating and relationships. By combining active listening, thoughtful questions, and playful energy, you can create conversations that leave a lasting impression. Remember, great communication isn't about impressing someone—it's about connecting with them on a deeper level.

In the next chapter, we'll explore the unspoken language of attraction: body language. Get ready to learn how to communicate desire without saying a word.

Chapter 7: Body Language Secrets: Speaking Without Words

In the dance of attraction, your body often speaks louder than your words. Before you even say a single thing, your body language communicates confidence, interest, and approachability. Men, consciously or unconsciously, pick up on these signals, and they often play a critical role in building chemistry.

Mastering body language doesn't mean faking who you are—it's about aligning your physical presence with your intentions. By understanding how to read and use non-verbal cues, you can project confidence, create intrigue, and subtly communicate your interest without needing to say a word.

This chapter explores the secrets of body language, teaching you how to exude magnetism and recognize the signals that men send in return.

7.1 Why Body Language Matters

Studies show that up to **93% of communication is non-verbal**, consisting of body language (55%) and tone of voice (38%). This means that your gestures, posture, and expressions are often more impactful than your words.

Here's why body language is so important in attraction:

- **It Creates Instant Impressions:** Your posture, facial expressions, and movements immediately tell someone how confident and open you are.

- **It Builds Tension:** Subtle, intentional gestures can create sexual tension and intrigue.

- **It Enhances Connection:** Mirroring someone's body language fosters a subconscious sense of connection and trust.

7.2 The Basics of Confident Body Language

To project confidence and captivate attention, start with these foundational elements:

1. Posture

Stand tall with your shoulders back and your head held high. Good posture conveys self-assurance and makes you appear more approachable.

Tips for Confident Posture:

- Keep your feet shoulder-width apart for a balanced stance.

- Avoid slouching or crossing your arms, which can make you seem closed off.

- Relax your shoulders to avoid looking tense or stiff.

2. Eye Contact

Eye contact is one of the most powerful tools for creating connection. Holding someone's gaze shows confidence and interest, while looking away too often can signal insecurity or disinterest.

Tips for Effective Eye Contact:

- Maintain eye contact for 3-5 seconds at a time, then look away naturally.

- Use a soft gaze instead of staring, which can feel intense.

- Pair eye contact with a warm smile to appear approachable.

3. Smiling

A genuine smile is inviting and disarming. It makes you appear friendly, warm, and open.

How to Use Your Smile:

- Start with a subtle smile when making eye contact, then let it grow naturally as the interaction progresses.

- Avoid forced or overly wide smiles, which can seem inauthentic.

- Practice smiling in the mirror to find a natural, relaxed expression.

7.3 Using Body Language to Show Interest

When you're attracted to someone, your body naturally leans toward them. You can amplify this effect intentionally to show interest and build a sense of intimacy.

How to Show Interest Through Body Language:

1. **Leaning In:** Subtly lean toward him during the conversation. This signals engagement and curiosity.

2. **Open Gestures:** Keep your arms relaxed and uncrossed. Use your hands to emphasize points or express enthusiasm.

3. **Mirroring:** Match his posture and gestures to create a subconscious connection. For example, if he leans on the table, do the same.

4. **Light Touches:** A gentle touch on his arm, shoulder, or hand can break the physical barrier and build a sense of closeness.

7.4 The Power of Subtle Movements

Small, deliberate movements can create intrigue and draw attention in a magnetic way.

Subtle Movements to Try:

- **Play with Your Hair:** Twirl a strand or lightly run your fingers through your hair, but avoid overdoing it.

- **Tilt Your Head:** Slightly tilting your head while listening shows engagement and curiosity.

- **Cross Your Legs Slowly:** If you're seated, crossing your legs slowly can add a touch of allure.

- **Use Your Hands Gracefully:** Whether holding a glass or gesturing while speaking, keep your movements fluid and intentional.

7.5 Reading His Body Language

Understanding a man's body language can help you gauge his level of interest and adjust your approach accordingly.

Signs He's Interested:

1. **He Mirrors Your Movements:** If he subconsciously copies your posture or gestures, it's a strong sign of connection.

2. **He Leans Toward You:** When a man leans in, he's signaling that he's engaged and attracted.

3. **He Faces You Fully:** If his torso, legs, and feet are pointed toward you, he's giving you his full attention.

4. **He Finds Excuses to Touch You:** Light, casual touches—like brushing your hand or tapping your arm—are signs he's testing the waters.

5. **He Maintains Eye Contact:** Sustained, warm eye contact often signals genuine interest.

Signs He's Not Interested:

- He avoids eye contact or frequently looks around the room.

- His body is angled away from you.

- He crosses his arms or creates physical distance.

- His responses are short or disengaged.

7.6 Creating Sexual Tension with Body Language

Sexual tension is the invisible energy that makes interactions thrilling. It's built through subtle, unspoken cues that create anticipation and desire.

How to Build Sexual Tension:

- **Hold Eye Contact Just a Little Longer:** Lock eyes for a few seconds longer than usual, then look away with a slight smile.

- **Play with Distance:** Lean in slightly as if you're about to whisper something, then pull back just enough to create a sense of longing.

- **Touch and Pause:** Lightly touch his arm or shoulder during the conversation, then withdraw to let the moment linger.

- **Speak Slowly and Softly:** Lowering your voice and slowing your speech can add intimacy to the interaction.

7.7 The Dos and Don'ts of Body Language

Dos:

- **Do Relax:** Relaxed movements and posture convey confidence and ease.

- **Do Smile Often:** Smiling makes you approachable and inviting.

- **Do Maintain Eye Contact:** It's the simplest way to create connection and build trust.

- **Do Mirror Subtly:** Mimicking his gestures shows alignment and interest.

Don'ts:

- **Don't Overdo Touching:** Excessive physical contact can feel overwhelming or insincere.

- **Don't Cross Your Arms:** This signals defensiveness or disinterest.

- **Don't Fidget:** Nervous habits like tapping your foot or playing with your phone can distract from the interaction.

- **Don't Be Too Rigid:** Stiff posture or forced movements can come across as unnatural.

7.8 Practical Exercises for Body Language Mastery

Exercise 1: Practice Your Posture

Stand in front of a mirror and practice standing tall with your shoulders back and your head high. Notice how this changes your energy and confidence.

Exercise 2: Eye Contact Drill

During your next few conversations, challenge yourself to hold eye contact for 3-5 seconds at a time before looking away. Gradually increase the duration to build comfort.

Exercise 3: Record Yourself

Record yourself speaking or moving. Pay attention to your gestures, posture, and expressions. Adjust anything that feels stiff or unnatural.

Conclusion

Body language is a powerful tool that allows you to communicate confidence, interest, and desire without saying a word. By mastering these non-verbal cues, you can create magnetic chemistry and deepen your connection with any man you meet. Remember, the key is to stay authentic—use these techniques to enhance your natural charm, not to hide it.

In the next chapter, we'll tackle one of the trickiest dynamics in relationships: breaking out of the friend zone and transforming platonic connections into romantic ones. Get ready to turn friendship into fireworks.

Chapter 8: Breaking the Friend Zone Barrier: Transforming Platonic Relationships Into Romance

The "friend zone" is a term that carries a mix of frustration and confusion, often leaving people wondering how they ended up there and whether they can ever escape. But the friend zone isn't a dead end—it's simply a dynamic that requires the right strategies to shift.

In this chapter, we'll dive into the art of breaking the friend zone barrier. Whether you've known someone for years or recently connected as friends, it's possible to transform a platonic relationship into a romantic one. You'll learn how to subtly change the dynamic, build attraction, and navigate the process with confidence and authenticity.

8.1 Understanding the Friend Zone

The friend zone occurs when one person feels romantically or sexually attracted to someone who only sees them as a friend. This often happens because the relationship becomes rooted in comfort, familiarity, and non-romantic patterns.

Why Do People End Up in the Friend Zone?

1. **Lack of Flirtation:** Without signals of attraction, the relationship can feel strictly platonic.

2. **Too Much Availability:** Always being there for someone can make them take you for granted.

3. **No Mystery:** When you're completely predictable, it can reduce intrigue and excitement.

4. **Misaligned Dynamics:** The other person may see you as a friend because that's how the relationship was framed from the beginning.

The good news? These dynamics can be shifted with the right approach.

8.2 Shifting the Dynamic: From Friend to Romantic Interest

Transforming a friendship into a romantic relationship starts with changing how the other person perceives you.

1. Change How You Present Yourself

One of the first steps is to elevate your appearance, energy, and confidence. This isn't about pretending to be someone you're not—it's about showcasing your most attractive qualities.

Action Steps:

- **Upgrade Your Style:** Wear outfits that make you feel confident and highlight your best features.

- **Work on Your Posture and Body Language:** Stand tall, smile often, and maintain eye contact to exude confidence.

- **Take Care of Yourself:** Physical and mental well-being play a huge role in how others perceive you.

2. Create Some Distance

If you've always been readily available to them, it's time to create a bit of space. This doesn't mean cutting them off—it means showing that you have your own life, passions, and priorities.

Action Steps:

- Be slightly less available than usual.

- Spend time with other friends or pursue hobbies that keep you busy.

- Let them notice that you're not always waiting in the wings.

Creating this distance can spark curiosity and make them start seeing you in a new light.

3. Introduce Flirtation

If your interactions have always been casual or friendly, it's time to sprinkle in some flirtation. This adds a layer of intrigue and subtly signals your interest.

Ways to Flirt with a Friend:

- Compliment them in a way that feels playful and romantic: "You look amazing today—why haven't I noticed that before?"

- Use touch sparingly, like a light touch on their arm or shoulder during a conversation.

- Playfully tease them: "I didn't know you had such a charming side—what else are you hiding?"

4. Start Creating Tension

Romantic tension is what differentiates a friendship from a romantic relationship. To build this tension, you need to create moments that feel different from your usual dynamic.

How to Build Tension:

- Make them laugh, but balance humor with moments of vulnerability.

- Hold eye contact slightly longer than usual.

- Lean in when talking, then subtly pull back to create anticipation.

8.3 Avoiding Common Friend Zone Pitfalls

When trying to transition out of the friend zone, it's important to avoid common mistakes that can sabotage your efforts.

1. Don't Overdo It

Sudden, dramatic changes in behavior can come off as inauthentic or awkward. Instead, focus on subtle, gradual shifts that feel natural.

2. Don't Confess Your Feelings Too Soon

A sudden declaration of love can overwhelm the other person, especially if they haven't started seeing you romantically yet. Instead, focus on building attraction first.

3. Don't Be Desperate

Desperation is a major turn-off. Remember that you're a catch, and your time and energy are valuable. Show them that you have standards and won't settle for less than mutual respect and interest.

8.4 Gauging Their Interest

Before taking things further, it's important to assess whether they're open to a romantic relationship. Pay attention to their actions and responses to your subtle advances.

Signs They Might Be Interested:

- They start complimenting you more or noticing things about your appearance.

- They initiate more conversations or want to spend more time with you.

- They respond positively to your flirtation, laughing or leaning into the moment.

- They ask about your dating life or hint at jealousy when you mention other people.

If you notice these signs, it's a good indication that they're starting to see you in a different light.

8.5 Taking the Next Step

Once you've established attraction and tension, it's time to move things forward.

1. Plan a One-on-One Hangout That Feels Like a Date

Shift the dynamic by suggesting an activity that feels more intimate than your usual outings. For example:

- "There's this new rooftop bar I've been dying to try—want to come with me?"

- "I'm in the mood for a movie night. Want to join me?"

Choose settings that encourage conversation and connection, like a cozy coffee shop, a wine bar, or a walk in the park.

2. Test the Waters

During your time together, increase the flirtation and physical closeness. For example, sit closer to them than usual, compliment their appearance, or hold their gaze. Notice how they respond.

3. Be Honest When the Moment Feels Right

If you sense that the feelings are mutual, it's okay to express your interest. Keep it simple and low-pressure:

- "I really enjoy spending time with you, and I feel like there's something more between us. What do you think?"

- "I have to admit, I've started seeing you in a different way lately. I feel like we might have something special."

Be prepared for their response—whether it's positive or hesitant—and respect their feelings.

8.6 What to Do If They Don't Feel the Same Way

Rejection can be difficult, but it doesn't have to ruin your friendship. If they don't share your feelings, handle the situation with grace and maturity.

How to Respond:

- **Stay Calm:** Thank them for their honesty and avoid getting defensive or upset.

- **Reassess the Friendship:** Decide whether you're comfortable staying friends or if you need some distance to move on.

- **Focus on Self-Growth:** Use the experience as an opportunity to learn and grow.

Remember, rejection doesn't define your worth. It simply means that person wasn't the right match for you romantically.

8.7 Practical Exercises for Breaking the Friend Zone

Exercise 1: Upgrade Your Presence

Choose one aspect of your appearance or demeanor to enhance—whether it's your style, posture, or energy. Notice how people respond to the change.

Exercise 2: Practice Flirting in Small Steps

The next time you hang out with your friend, add one subtle flirtation technique, like a compliment or playful tease. See how they react and adjust accordingly.

Exercise 3: Build Emotional Intimacy

Share something personal with your friend that you haven't discussed before. Vulnerability helps deepen your connection and shift the dynamic.

Conclusion

Breaking out of the friend zone requires patience, subtlety, and self-confidence. By changing the way you present yourself, introducing flirtation, and building romantic tension, you can shift the dynamic and open the door to a deeper connection. Remember, the key is to stay authentic and true to yourself—romantic interest should feel natural and mutual, not forced.

In the next chapter, we'll explore how to craft an irresistible aura that makes you unforgettable, whether you're building a new relationship or strengthening an existing one.

Chapter 9: Crafting an Irresistible Aura: Becoming the Woman Every Man Desires

Attraction isn't just about looks or clever words—it's about the energy you project. Your aura is the intangible, magnetic quality that makes people want to be around you. It's the confidence, positivity, and authenticity that leave a lasting impression long after you've left the room.

In this chapter, we'll explore how to cultivate an irresistible aura that draws men in naturally. This is about becoming the best version of yourself—inside and out—so you can attract the men you desire without effort or pretense.

9.1 What Is an Irresistible Aura?

An irresistible aura is the unique energy and vibe that makes you stand out. It's not about being perfect but about being captivating in your own way. Men are drawn to women who exude confidence, warmth, and authenticity because these qualities create a sense of comfort and intrigue.

Key Elements of an Irresistible Aura:

- **Confidence:** Believing in yourself and knowing your worth.

- **Positivity:** Radiating joy and optimism that uplifts others.

- **Authenticity:** Being true to yourself and comfortable in your own skin.

- **Mystery:** Leaving something to the imagination and keeping people curious about you.

9.2 Building Confidence from Within

Confidence is the foundation of your aura. It's what allows you to walk into a room and command attention without saying a word.

How to Build Inner Confidence:

1. **Celebrate Your Strengths:** Write down your best qualities—physical, emotional, and intellectual—and remind yourself of them often.

2. **Silence Negative Self-Talk:** Replace thoughts like, "I'm not good enough," with affirmations like, "I have so much to offer."

3. **Step Out of Your Comfort Zone:** Growth happens when you challenge yourself. Try new experiences that help you build resilience and self-assurance.

4. **Prioritize Self-Care:** When you take care of your physical and emotional well-being, you naturally feel more confident.

9.3 Cultivating Positivity

A positive attitude is magnetic. People are drawn to those who make them feel good, and your outlook on life plays a huge role in the energy you project.

Tips for Radiating Positivity:

- **Practice Gratitude:** Focus on what's going well in your life and express thanks for the small joys each day.

- **Smile Often:** A genuine smile can brighten your energy and make you more approachable.

- **Be Playful:** Don't take life too seriously—find humor in everyday moments and share your laughter with others.

- **Focus on Solutions:** Instead of dwelling on problems, look for ways to overcome challenges. This optimism is inspiring to others.

9.4 Authenticity: The Heart of Your Aura

There's nothing more attractive than someone who is unapologetically themselves. Authenticity means embracing your quirks, values, and passions without fear of judgment.

How to Be Authentically You:

1. **Know Your Values:** What matters most to you? Let your actions and choices reflect these priorities.

2. **Express Yourself:** Don't be afraid to share your opinions, interests, or sense of humor, even if they're unique.

3. **Let Go of People-Pleasing:** You don't need to mold yourself to fit someone else's expectations. The right people will love you for who you are.

9.5 Adding a Touch of Mystery

Mystery isn't about hiding who you are—it's about keeping an air of intrigue that makes people want to know more about you.

Ways to Cultivate Mystery:

- **Don't Overshare:** Let people discover you gradually. For example, hint at an interesting story but save the details for later.

- **Be Slightly Unpredictable:** Switch up your routines and surprise people with unexpected ideas or plans.

- **Leave Them Wanting More:** End conversations or interactions on a high note, so they're left thinking about you.

9.6 The Power of Presence

Being fully present in the moment is a rare and powerful quality. When you give someone your undivided attention, it makes them feel valued and creates a deeper connection.

How to Be Present:

- **Put Away Distractions:** When you're with someone, focus entirely on them. Avoid checking your phone or letting your mind wander.

- **Listen Intently:** Pay attention to their words, tone, and body language. Respond thoughtfully to show you're engaged.

- **Savor the Moment:** Whether you're having a conversation, sharing a meal, or simply walking together, enjoy the experience fully.

9.7 Building an Irresistible Outer Presence

While your inner confidence and energy are crucial, how you present yourself externally also plays a role in your aura.

Tips for Enhancing Your Outer Presence:

1. **Dress for Confidence:** Wear clothes that make you feel powerful and reflect your personality.

2. **Grooming Matters:** A polished appearance shows self-respect and attention to detail.

3. **Practice Graceful Movements:** Move with purpose and poise, whether you're walking, sitting, or gesturing.

4. **Experiment with Signature Details:** A signature perfume, hairstyle, or accessory can make you memorable.

9.8 How Your Aura Attracts the Right Men

An irresistible aura doesn't just attract attention—it filters for the right kind of attention. When you embody confidence, positivity, and authenticity, you naturally draw men who are aligned with your values and energy.

Why Your Aura Matters:

- It shows that you value yourself, which encourages others to value you too.

- It signals that you're not desperate for validation, making you more intriguing.

- It creates a sense of comfort and excitement that makes people want to be around you.

9.9 Practical Exercises to Develop Your Aura

Exercise 1: The "Power Pose" Practice

Every morning, stand in a power pose for two minutes—feet shoulder-width apart, hands on your hips, shoulders back, and chin up. This boosts your confidence and sets the tone for the day.

Exercise 2: Daily Gratitude List

Write down three things you're grateful for each day. This simple habit shifts your focus to positivity and helps you radiate joy.

Exercise 3: Compliment Others

Give at least one genuine compliment each day. This builds your confidence in connecting with others and makes you more magnetic.

Exercise 4: Mirror Work

Stand in front of a mirror and practice smiling, holding eye contact, and speaking affirmations like, "I am confident, radiant, and irresistible."

Conclusion

Your aura is the essence of who you are—it's the combination of your confidence, energy, and authenticity that makes you unforgettable. By cultivating a positive, self-assured presence, you can attract the men you desire effortlessly. Remember, an irresistible aura isn't about pretending to be someone you're not—it's about amplifying the best parts of who you already are.

In the next chapter, we'll focus on navigating the crucial first date, where you'll learn how to build connection, create sexual tension, and leave a lasting impression that keeps him wanting more.

Chapter 10: Navigating the First Date: Building Connection and Sexual Tension

The first date is a pivotal moment in any romantic journey—it's your chance to build a genuine connection, create sparks, and leave a lasting impression. Whether you met him through friends, online, or during one of your confident approaches, the first date sets the tone for what's to come.

In this chapter, we'll dive into how to prepare for a first date, navigate the conversation, and strike the perfect balance between emotional connection and sexual tension. With the right mindset and strategies, you can transform a casual outing into the beginning of something meaningful—or at least make it an unforgettable experience.

10.1 The Mindset of a Successful First Date

Before you even step out the door, it's important to approach the first date with the right mindset. Instead of focusing on whether he'll like you, shift your perspective to whether *you* like him. This subtle change empowers you and takes the pressure off.

The Goals of a First Date:

1. **Enjoy Yourself:** Focus on having fun and being in the moment.

2. **Assess Compatibility:** Use the time to determine if he aligns with your values and interests.

3. **Create Chemistry:** Build a connection that leaves both of you wanting more.

Adopting a Confident Mindset:

- Remind yourself of your worth—this date is about discovering if *he* deserves *you*.

- Focus on the experience, not the outcome. Even if he's not a match, it's an opportunity to practice your dating skills.

- Let go of perfection—authenticity is far more attractive than trying to impress.

10.2 Preparing for the First Date

A little preparation can go a long way in setting you up for success.

What to Wear:

Your outfit should reflect your personality and make you feel confident. Choose something that flatters your figure, is appropriate for the setting, and makes you feel amazing.

- **Casual Date:** Jeans with a fitted top or a casual dress paired with stylish accessories.

- **Dinner Date:** A chic dress or a blouse with tailored pants and heels.

- **Active Date:** Comfortable yet flattering athleisure or casual wear.

What to Bring:

- **An Open Mind:** Be ready to enjoy the moment, even if things don't go as planned.

- **A Positive Attitude:** Enthusiasm and warmth make a great impression.

- **Light Conversation Topics:** Have a few fun or engaging questions in mind to avoid awkward silences.

Pre-Date Rituals:

- Spend some time getting ready while listening to music that boosts your confidence.

- Practice deep breathing to calm any nerves.

- Look in the mirror and remind yourself, "I'm confident, radiant, and worth knowing."

10.3 The Art of Conversation on a First Date

Conversation is the heart of a successful first date. It's your opportunity to connect on a deeper level while keeping the mood light and enjoyable.

Tips for Engaging Conversation:

1. **Start with Light Topics:** Begin with easy, upbeat questions to break the ice. For example:

   o "What's the best thing that's happened to you this week?"

   o "If you could have dinner with any historical figure, who would it be?"
2. **Ask Open-Ended Questions:** These encourage more meaningful responses. For example:

   o "What's something you're really passionate about?"

   o "What's a goal you're working toward right now?"

3. **Share Stories:** Don't just ask questions—contribute your own stories and insights to make the conversation feel balanced.

4. **Use Playful Teasing:** A little banter adds fun and chemistry. For example:

    o "I don't know if I trust someone who doesn't like chocolate—are you sure we can be friends?"

5. **Stay Present:** Listen actively, maintain eye contact, and avoid distractions like your phone.

10.4 Building Emotional Connection

To make a lasting impression, focus on creating a sense of emotional intimacy.

How to Build Connection:

- **Be Curious:** Show genuine interest in his experiences, values, and dreams.

- **Find Common Ground:** Highlight shared interests or experiences to create a sense of familiarity.

- **Share Vulnerabilities:** When appropriate, open up about something personal—this builds trust and closeness. For example: "One of the biggest challenges I faced taught me so much about myself…"

10.5 Creating Sexual Tension on a First Date

Sexual tension is the subtle, electric current that turns a pleasant evening into something unforgettable. It's about building attraction in a way that feels natural and exciting.

Tips for Building Sexual Tension:

1. **Flirt with Eye Contact:** Hold his gaze for a second longer than usual, then look away with a slight smile.

2. **Playful Touches:** Lightly touch his hand, arm, or shoulder during conversation to create physical closeness.

3. **Compliment Him:** Make your compliments personal and slightly flirtatious. For example: "You have such a confident energy—it's really attractive."

4. **Lean In:** When the conversation becomes more personal or intimate, subtly lean toward him to signal interest.

5. **Use Your Voice:** Speak softly and slowly when the moment feels right, adding a sense of intimacy to your words.

10.6 Ending the Date on a High Note

How you end the date is just as important as how it begins. Leaving him with a positive impression ensures he'll be thinking about you long after you've said goodbye.

How to End the Date Gracefully:

1. **Express Gratitude:** Thank him for the date and acknowledge something you enjoyed. For example, "I had a great time—it was so fun getting to know you."

2. **Signal Your Interest (If You're Interested):** If you'd like to see him again, drop a hint. For example: "We should do this again sometime—I'd love to hear more about [something he mentioned]."

3. **Keep It Classy:** If the date went well but you're not ready to take things further physically, a warm hug or kiss on the cheek can convey your interest without rushing.

10.7 Handling Awkward Moments

Not every first date will go perfectly, and that's okay. How you handle awkward moments shows grace and emotional intelligence.

Common Awkward Moments and How to Handle Them:

- **Awkward Silences:** Acknowledge it playfully with something like, "Well, that was a dramatic pause—your turn!"

- **If the Chemistry Isn't There:** Stay polite and positive, but don't feel pressured to pursue something that doesn't feel right.

- **If He Says Something Off-Putting:** Respond with kindness but hold your boundaries. For example, "I see where you're coming from, but I don't think I agree with that."

10.8 Practical Exercises for First Date Confidence

Exercise 1: Visualization

Before your date, close your eyes and visualize yourself walking in confidently, enjoying the conversation, and having a great time. This helps reduce anxiety and sets a positive tone.

Exercise 2: Mirror Practice

Practice smiling, making eye contact, and introducing yourself in front of a mirror. This helps you feel more comfortable and prepared.

Exercise 3: Gratitude Journal

Before the date, write down three things you're grateful for to shift your mindset to one of positivity and abundance.

Conclusion

The first date is your chance to showcase your confidence, build a meaningful connection, and create sparks of chemistry. By preparing thoughtfully, engaging in captivating conversation, and adding a touch of flirtation, you can ensure the date is memorable for both of you.

In the next chapter, we'll explore how to keep him hooked after the first date by deepening the emotional bond and maintaining the intrigue. Get ready to learn the art of keeping the connection alive and thriving.

Chapter 11: Keeping Him Hooked: The Keys to Emotional Bonding

The first date might ignite the spark, but the real magic happens in the days and weeks that follow. Once you've captured his attention and left a positive impression, the next step is to deepen the emotional connection. Emotional bonding is what keeps a man hooked and invested in you. It's the glue that turns infatuation into genuine interest and attraction into commitment.

In this chapter, we'll uncover the secrets to nurturing a meaningful connection, building trust, and maintaining intrigue while fostering a relationship that feels fresh, exciting, and real.

11.1 The Foundation of Emotional Bonding

Emotional bonding goes beyond surface-level attraction. It's about creating a space where both of you feel seen, valued, and safe to be yourselves.

The Core Elements of Emotional Bonding:

1. **Trust:** The cornerstone of any strong connection. Trust develops when you show consistency, honesty, and respect.

2. **Vulnerability:** Sharing your thoughts, fears, and dreams creates intimacy.

3. **Mutual Appreciation:** Both partners need to feel valued and appreciated for who they are.

4. **Empathy:** Understanding and validating each other's emotions strengthens the bond.

Building these elements takes time and effort, but they're essential for a lasting connection.

11.2 Communicating to Build a Deeper Connection

Clear, honest communication is one of the most effective ways to keep a man emotionally invested. It's not just about talking—it's about truly connecting.

Tips for Effective Communication:

1. **Ask Thoughtful Questions:** Show genuine curiosity about his life, dreams, and challenges. For example:

   o "What's something you've always wanted to do but haven't yet?"

   o "What's the most important lesson you've learned this year?"

2. **Listen Actively:** Pay attention to his words and emotions, and respond in a way that shows you understand.

3. **Share Your World:** Let him see your passions, values, and aspirations. When you open up, he'll feel encouraged to do the same.

4. **Express Appreciation:** Acknowledge the things you admire about him, whether it's his sense of humor, work ethic, or kindness.

11.3 Balancing Intimacy and Independence

One of the biggest mistakes people make in the early stages of a relationship is losing their sense of self. While it's natural to want to spend time together, maintaining your independence is key to keeping the relationship healthy and exciting.

How to Maintain Balance:

- **Pursue Your Passions:** Continue to invest in your hobbies, goals, and friendships. A fulfilled life outside the relationship makes you more attractive and gives you more to share.

- **Set Healthy Boundaries:** Don't feel pressured to be available 24/7. Time apart creates room for both of you to miss and appreciate each other.

- **Encourage His Independence:** Support his interests and activities, even if they don't involve you. A secure relationship thrives on mutual trust and freedom.

11.4 Keeping the Relationship Fresh and Exciting

Routine can dull the spark in any relationship, but with a little effort, you can keep things fresh and exciting.

Ways to Keep Him Hooked:

1. **Plan Surprises:** Surprise him with small gestures, like leaving a sweet note or planning a fun outing.

2. **Be Spontaneous:** Try new activities together, whether it's cooking a new recipe, exploring a new part of town, or going on an impromptu road trip.

3. **Keep Flirting:** Just because the first date is over doesn't mean the playful banter has to stop. Keep the chemistry alive with compliments, teasing, and light touches.

4. **Focus on Growth:** Encourage each other to grow individually and as a couple. Celebrate milestones, set shared goals, and support each other's dreams.

11.5 Creating Emotional Safety

Emotional safety is the feeling that you can be yourself without fear of judgment or rejection. It's what allows both partners to open up and build a deep connection.

How to Create Emotional Safety:

- **Be Honest:** Share your thoughts and feelings openly, and encourage him to do the same.

- **Avoid Criticism:** If you need to address an issue, focus on solutions rather than blaming or criticizing.

- **Show Understanding:** Even if you don't agree with his perspective, acknowledge his feelings and validate his experiences.

- **Be Consistent:** Reliability builds trust. Follow through on your promises and show that he can depend on you.

11.6 Recognizing His Efforts

Men, like anyone else, want to feel valued and appreciated. Acknowledging his efforts, no matter how small, makes him feel seen and motivates him to continue investing in the relationship.

How to Show Appreciation:

- **Say Thank You:** Whether he plans a date, helps you with something, or simply listens, express your gratitude.

- **Notice the Little Things:** Compliment his thoughtfulness, humor, or the way he makes you feel. For example, "I love how you always make me laugh, even on tough days."

- **Reciprocate Thoughtfulness:** If he does something nice for you, find a way to do something kind for him in return.

11.7 The Role of Mystery in Long-Term Attraction

While emotional intimacy is crucial, maintaining a sense of intrigue can keep the spark alive. When a man feels like there's always something new to discover about you, he'll stay curious and engaged.

How to Maintain Mystery:

- **Keep Evolving:** Continuously pursue your interests, learn new skills, and set new goals. A woman who's always growing is endlessly fascinating.

- **Don't Overshare:** While it's important to be open, save some stories or experiences for later. Let him uncover different layers of you over time.

- **Surprise Him:** Occasionally break the routine by doing something unexpected, whether it's planning a surprise date or sharing a hidden talent.

11.8 Recognizing Red Flags Early

As you deepen the connection, it's essential to stay aware of any red flags that might indicate the relationship isn't healthy.

Common Red Flags to Watch For:

- **Lack of Effort:** If he doesn't invest time or energy into the relationship, it may signal disinterest.

- **Inconsistency:** Pay attention to whether his words align with his actions.

- **Avoidance of Emotional Intimacy:** If he struggles to open up or avoids serious conversations, it could indicate emotional unavailability.

- **Controlling Behavior:** Healthy relationships are built on mutual respect and freedom, not control or manipulation.

If you notice these red flags, address them directly and decide whether the relationship is worth pursuing.

11.9 Practical Exercises to Deepen Emotional Bonding

Exercise 1: Gratitude Exchange

At the end of the day, take a moment to share something you're grateful for about each other. For example, "I really appreciated how you made me laugh today—it meant a lot."

Exercise 2: Dream Sharing

Spend time talking about your dreams and aspirations. Ask questions like, "What's something you've always wanted to achieve?" or "Where do you see yourself in five years?"

Exercise 3: Plan a Shared Experience

Choose an activity that neither of you has tried before and do it together. New experiences create lasting memories and strengthen your bond.

Conclusion

Keeping a man hooked isn't about playing games or changing who you are—it's about building an emotional connection that's rooted in trust, vulnerability, and mutual appreciation. By communicating openly, maintaining your independence, and nurturing the relationship with care and creativity, you can create a bond that stands the test of time.

In the next chapter, we'll shift focus to navigating the transition from casual to committed, giving you the tools to secure the relationship you want without forcing it.

Chapter 12: From Casual to Committed: How to Secure the Relationship You Want

One of the most crucial transitions in any romantic journey is moving from casual dating to a committed relationship. While some connections naturally progress in that direction, others require clarity, communication, and intentional effort.

In this chapter, we'll explore how to guide the relationship into commitment without forcing it. You'll learn how to communicate your desires, recognize signs he's ready (or not), and navigate the delicate balance between patience and action. Ultimately, this chapter is about ensuring that the relationship evolves in a way that feels organic, fulfilling, and aligned with your goals.

12.1 Understanding the Transition from Casual to Committed

Casual dating often involves exploration, where both people are figuring out whether they're compatible and aligned. Commitment, on the other hand, involves exclusivity, trust, and long-term investment in each other.

What Commitment Means:

1. **Emotional Investment:** Both partners are deeply engaged in each other's lives.

2. **Exclusivity:** The relationship becomes a priority over other romantic or casual connections.

3. **Shared Vision:** Both partners are aligned in their values, goals, and expectations for the future.

The transition happens naturally when both people feel secure, connected, and excited about building something lasting.

12.2 Signs He's Ready for Commitment

Before initiating a conversation about commitment, it's important to gauge whether he's already moving in that direction.

Signs He's Ready:

1. **He Prioritizes You:** He consistently makes time for you and values your presence in his life.

2. **He Introduces You to His Inner Circle:** Meeting his friends or family is often a sign he's serious about the relationship.

3. **He Talks About the Future:** If he includes you in his plans or talks about long-term goals, it's a strong indication he sees you as part of his life.

4. **He Shows Consistency:** His actions align with his words, and he's reliable and dependable.

5. **He Asks About Your Desires:** If he's curious about what you want in a relationship, it's a sign he's considering taking things to the next level.

12.3 Communicating Your Desires

If you feel ready for commitment but the relationship hasn't naturally transitioned yet, it's important to express your desires clearly and calmly.

How to Bring Up the Conversation:

1. **Choose the Right Time:** Avoid initiating serious discussions during moments of stress or distraction. Instead, pick a time when you're both relaxed and engaged.

2. **Start with Positivity:** Begin the conversation by expressing how much you value the relationship. For example:

    o "I've really enjoyed spending time with you, and I feel like we have a great connection."

3. **Be Clear and Direct:** Share your feelings and what you're looking for. For example:

    o "I'm at a point where I'm looking for something more serious, and I want to make sure we're on the same page."

4. **Invite His Perspective:** Give him space to share his thoughts and feelings. For example:

    o "How do you feel about where we're headed?"

Dos and Don'ts of the Commitment Talk:

- **Do:** Focus on your feelings and desires rather than making demands.

- **Don't:** Ultimatums can create pressure and resentment. Instead, foster an open and honest dialogue.

- **Do:** Be prepared for his response, whether it's positive or hesitant.

- **Don't:** Let fear of rejection keep you from expressing your truth.

12.4 When He's Hesitant About Commitment

Not every man is ready for commitment at the same time. If he's hesitant, it doesn't necessarily mean he's not interested—it could be due to personal fears, past experiences, or a need for more time.

How to Handle Hesitation:

1. **Ask Open-Ended Questions:** Understand what's holding him back. For example:

   o "What are your thoughts on commitment? Is there something you're worried about?"

2. **Give Him Time:** If he's genuinely interested in you but needs more time, consider whether you're willing to wait. Set a personal timeline for how long you're comfortable being patient.

3. **Reaffirm Your Boundaries:** While it's okay to give him time, don't compromise your own needs indefinitely. For example:

   o "I understand that you need time, but I also want to make sure I'm honoring what I'm looking for."

12.5 Creating an Environment That Fosters Commitment

Sometimes, actions speak louder than words. Creating a relationship dynamic that feels secure, exciting, and supportive can naturally encourage commitment.

How to Foster Commitment:

1. **Be His Safe Space:** Offer emotional support, understanding, and acceptance.

2. **Maintain Your Independence:** Continue pursuing your own goals, hobbies, and friendships. A partner who sees you as self-sufficient and fulfilled will feel more inspired to invest in you.

3. **Build Shared Memories:** Create experiences that strengthen your bond, such as traveling together, trying new activities, or celebrating milestones.

4. **Express Appreciation:** Regularly show gratitude for the things he does, whether big or small.

12.6 Recognizing When It's Time to Walk Away

Sometimes, no matter how much effort you put into a relationship, it may become clear that he's not ready or willing to commit. Knowing when to walk away is essential for protecting your emotional well-being.

Signs It's Time to Move On:

- He avoids discussions about the future or consistently changes the subject.

- He's inconsistent in his actions and doesn't prioritize the relationship.

- He openly states that he doesn't want a committed relationship when you've expressed that you do.

- You feel like you're always waiting for him to change without seeing progress.

Walking away can be painful, but it also creates space for someone who shares your vision for the future.

12.7 Practical Exercises to Prepare for Commitment Conversations

Exercise 1: Reflect on Your Values

Write down what you're looking for in a committed relationship. Identify your non-negotiables, such as exclusivity, shared goals, or communication styles.

Exercise 2: Practice the Talk

Rehearse how you'd bring up the commitment conversation with a friend or in front of a mirror. Focus on expressing yourself calmly and clearly.

Exercise 3: Set Boundaries for Yourself

Decide how long you're willing to wait for him to commit. Write down your boundaries and remind yourself to honor them if the relationship isn't progressing.

Conclusion

Transitioning from casual to committed is a delicate yet rewarding process that requires clarity, communication, and mutual investment. By expressing your desires honestly, fostering an environment of trust and connection, and respecting your own boundaries, you can navigate this stage with confidence.

In the next chapter, we'll dive into identifying red flags and protecting yourself from relationships that don't align with your needs, ensuring you stay on the path to love and fulfillment.

Chapter 13: Recognizing Red Flags: Identifying and Avoiding the Wrong Men

While dating and building relationships can be exciting, it's essential to stay vigilant about potential red flags. Red flags are warning signs that someone may not be a good fit for you or may lack the emotional capacity to build a healthy, fulfilling relationship. Recognizing these signs early can save you from heartache and wasted time, empowering you to make choices that align with your values and desires.

This chapter will help you identify common red flags, understand how to address them, and decide when it's time to walk away. You deserve a relationship built on trust, respect, and mutual effort, and this guide will help you avoid settling for anything less.

13.1 Why It's Important to Recognize Red Flags

Ignoring red flags often leads to frustration, resentment, and toxic relationship dynamics. While no one is perfect, certain behaviors and patterns signal deeper issues that can harm your emotional well-being. By identifying these signs early, you can make informed decisions about whether to invest in the relationship or move on.

What Ignoring Red Flags Can Lead To:

1. **Emotional Exhaustion:** Constantly dealing with unhealthy behaviors drains your energy.

2. **Loss of Self-Worth:** Being in a relationship with someone who disrespects you can chip away at your confidence.

3. **Wasted Time:** Investing in the wrong person keeps you from finding someone who truly aligns with your values.

Remember, paying attention to red flags isn't about being overly critical—it's about protecting your heart and honoring your needs.

13.2 Common Red Flags in Dating

1. Lack of Communication

Healthy relationships thrive on open and honest communication. If he avoids discussing feelings, dismisses your concerns, or shuts down when conflicts arise, it's a sign he may not be emotionally mature or willing to invest in the relationship.

What to Look For:

- He avoids serious conversations or changes the subject.
- He refuses to take accountability for his actions.
- He becomes defensive or dismissive when you express your needs.

---

2. Inconsistency

Consistency is a cornerstone of trust. If his behavior, words, or actions are unpredictable, it can create confusion and insecurity in the relationship.

What to Look For:

- He's hot and cold—one day he's attentive, the next he's distant.
- He makes promises but rarely follows through.
- His actions don't align with his words.

---

3. Disrespect for Boundaries

A man who disrespects your boundaries, whether emotional, physical, or personal, shows a lack of regard for your needs and autonomy.

What to Look For:

- He pressures you into things you're not comfortable with.
- He dismisses your opinions or belittles your decisions.
- He invades your privacy or disregards your requests.

---

4. Excessive Jealousy or Control

While mild jealousy can be normal, excessive jealousy or controlling behavior is a red flag for insecurity and possessiveness.

What to Look For:

- He constantly questions your whereabouts or who you're with.
- He tries to control how you dress, who you see, or what you do.
- He becomes angry or withdrawn if you assert your independence.

---

5. Lack of Effort

A healthy relationship requires mutual effort. If he's not putting in the work to build a connection, it may indicate disinterest or selfishness.

What to Look For:

- He rarely initiates dates, plans, or meaningful conversations.

- He expects you to do all the emotional labor, like solving conflicts or keeping the relationship going.

- He doesn't prioritize you or the relationship.

6. Past Relationship Patterns

His history with past relationships can provide valuable insights into his emotional readiness. If he has a pattern of toxic relationships, unresolved issues, or an inability to commit, it's worth paying attention.

What to Look For:

- He constantly bad-mouths his exes or blames them for everything.

- He has a history of infidelity or commitment issues.

- He jumps quickly from one relationship to the next without taking time to reflect.

7. Emotional Unavailability

A man who's emotionally unavailable may struggle to connect, share his feelings, or invest in a relationship.

What to Look For:

- He avoids vulnerability or deep conversations.

- He keeps you at arm's length and doesn't let you into his life.

- He makes excuses for why he can't commit or prioritize the relationship.

13.3 How to Address Red Flags

If you notice red flags, it's important to address them directly rather than ignoring or excusing them. Honest communication can help you determine whether the issue is fixable or a dealbreaker.

Steps to Address Red Flags:

1. **Acknowledge the Behavior:** Calmly bring up the behavior that's concerning you. For example:

   o "I've noticed that you avoid talking about certain things, and I want to understand why."

2. **Ask Questions:** Seek clarity about his perspective. For example:

   o "Can you explain what's going on? I want to make sure we're on the same page."

3. **Set Boundaries:** Clearly communicate your expectations and limits. For example:

   o "I need a partner who respects my boundaries and communicates openly."

4. **Observe His Response:** Pay attention to how he reacts. Does he take accountability and make an effort to improve, or does he dismiss your concerns?

13.4 When to Walk Away

While some issues can be resolved through communication and mutual effort, others are clear signs that it's time to end the relationship.

Non-Negotiable Red Flags:

- **Abuse (Emotional, Physical, or Verbal):** Abuse in any form is unacceptable and dangerous.

- **Chronic Dishonesty:** If he lies frequently, trust will be impossible to build.

- **Repeated Boundary Violations:** A partner who disregards your boundaries shows a lack of respect.

Walking away can be difficult, especially if you've invested time and emotion, but it's essential for your well-being. Trust that letting go creates space for someone who values and respects you.

13.5 Trusting Your Intuition

Your gut feeling is a powerful tool when it comes to recognizing red flags. If something feels off, don't dismiss it. Take time to reflect on your feelings and seek input from trusted friends or family.

Questions to Ask Yourself:

- Do I feel respected and valued in this relationship?
- Am I constantly questioning his actions or intentions?
- Does this relationship align with my values and goals?

If the answer to these questions is no, it's worth reassessing whether the relationship is right for you.

13.6 Practical Exercises for Recognizing and Avoiding Red Flags

Exercise 1: Create a Non-Negotiables List

Write down your dealbreakers in a relationship—behaviors or traits that you won't tolerate. Keep this list in mind as you evaluate potential partners.

Exercise 2: Reflect on Past Relationships

Think about past relationships and identify any red flags you overlooked. Use these insights to recognize patterns and avoid similar situations in the future.

Exercise 3: Roleplay Difficult Conversations

Practice addressing red flags with a friend or in front of a mirror. This helps you build confidence in expressing your concerns calmly and assertively.

Conclusion

Recognizing red flags is essential for protecting your heart and building a relationship that aligns with your values. While no one is perfect, you deserve a partner who respects you, communicates openly, and invests in your happiness. Trust yourself to walk away from situations that don't serve you and hold out for the love you truly deserve.

In the next chapter, we'll explore how to sustain passion and intimacy in a long-term relationship, ensuring that the connection remains vibrant and fulfilling.

Chapter 14: Sustaining Passion and Intimacy: Long-Term Seduction Strategies

The early stages of a relationship are often filled with excitement, passion, and a sense of discovery. But as time goes on, maintaining that spark requires intention and effort. Passion and intimacy don't fade because they have to—they fade because they're neglected. The good news is that with the right approach, you can keep the fire alive and even deepen your connection over time.

In this chapter, we'll explore strategies for sustaining passion and intimacy in a long-term relationship. From keeping romance alive to deepening emotional and physical connection, these tips will help you create a partnership that remains vibrant, exciting, and fulfilling.

14.1 Why Passion Fades in Long-Term Relationships

It's natural for relationships to evolve over time. The initial rush of infatuation—driven by novelty and curiosity—eventually gives way to comfort and routine. While this shift can strengthen emotional intimacy, it can also lead to complacency if both partners stop putting in the effort to nurture the relationship.

Common Reasons Passion Fades:

1. **Routine Overrules Romance:** Daily responsibilities and habits take precedence over connection.

2. **Lack of Novelty:** When the relationship becomes predictable, the excitement diminishes.

3. **Emotional Distance:** Unresolved conflicts or lack of communication create barriers to intimacy.

4. **Physical Neglect:** Intimacy wanes when partners stop prioritizing physical affection and connection.

The key to sustaining passion is recognizing these challenges and addressing them proactively.

14.2 The Pillars of Long-Term Passion and Intimacy

Maintaining passion in a long-term relationship requires a balance of emotional, physical, and romantic connection.

1. Emotional Intimacy

Emotional closeness is the foundation of a lasting relationship. When both partners feel understood and valued, it strengthens the bond and creates a safe space for passion to thrive.

How to Foster Emotional Intimacy:

- **Have Regular Check-Ins:** Set aside time to discuss how you're feeling about the relationship and any challenges you're facing.

- **Be Vulnerable:** Share your dreams, fears, and innermost thoughts. Letting your guard down deepens the connection.

- **Show Appreciation:** Express gratitude for your partner's efforts, both big and small.

2. Physical Connection

Physical intimacy is an essential component of passion. It's not just about sex—it's about touch, affection, and the small moments of physical closeness that reinforce your bond.

How to Maintain Physical Intimacy:

- **Prioritize Affection:** Hold hands, hug, kiss, and cuddle regularly to keep the connection alive.

- **Be Playful:** Surprise your partner with a kiss in the kitchen or a flirty touch when passing by.

- **Explore Together:** Keep your sex life exciting by trying new things and openly communicating about your desires.

3. Romantic Effort

Romance isn't just for the beginning of a relationship—it's a lifelong practice that keeps the spark alive.

How to Keep Romance Alive:

- **Plan Date Nights:** Regularly dedicate time to enjoy each other's company without distractions.

- **Surprise Each Other:** Small, thoughtful gestures—like leaving a note or planning a surprise outing—go a long way.

- **Revisit Special Moments:** Reminisce about your first date, recreate meaningful experiences, or look through old photos together.

14.3 Injecting Novelty into Your Relationship

One of the most effective ways to reignite passion is by introducing novelty into the relationship. New experiences stimulate the brain's reward system, creating excitement and a sense of adventure.

Ideas for Adding Novelty:

1. **Try Something New Together:** Take a cooking class, go hiking, or learn a new hobby as a couple.

2. **Travel to a New Destination:** Exploring new places together strengthens your bond and creates lasting memories.

3. **Switch Up Your Routine:** Break out of your usual patterns—try a new restaurant, rearrange your living space, or plan an unexpected date.

14.4 Strengthening Emotional and Physical Communication

Communication is the bridge between emotional and physical intimacy. When you understand each other's needs and desires, it becomes easier to sustain a fulfilling connection.

How to Strengthen Communication:

- **Talk About Intimacy:** Have open and honest conversations about what makes each of you feel desired and loved.

- **Practice Active Listening:** Truly hear your partner's concerns or desires without interrupting or becoming defensive.

- **Use Affirming Words:** Compliment your partner, express your love, and remind them of how much they mean to you.

14.5 Managing Conflict to Preserve Intimacy

Conflict is inevitable in any relationship, but how you handle it can either strengthen or weaken your bond. Unresolved conflicts often lead to resentment, which can erode passion over time.

Healthy Ways to Handle Conflict:

1. **Address Issues Early:** Don't let small frustrations fester—talk about them before they grow into larger problems.

2. **Focus on Solutions:** Instead of assigning blame, work together to find a resolution.

3. **Apologize and Forgive:** Take responsibility for your mistakes and be willing to forgive your partner's.

Managing conflict effectively creates a sense of security and trust, which are essential for sustaining intimacy.

14.6 The Role of Playfulness in Long-Term Passion

Playfulness isn't just for the honeymoon phase—it's a powerful tool for keeping your relationship fun and exciting.

Ways to Be Playful Together:

- **Flirt Daily:** Send flirty texts, tease each other, or give compliments that make them blush.

- **Laugh Together:** Watch a comedy, tell silly jokes, or reminisce about funny moments you've shared.

- **Be Spontaneous:** Surprise your partner with an impromptu dance in the living room or a spontaneous road trip.

Playfulness reminds you both to enjoy the lighter side of life and keeps the relationship fresh.

14.7 Overcoming Common Challenges to Long-Term Passion

Every relationship faces challenges, but addressing them with intention can help you overcome obstacles and strengthen your bond.

Common Challenges and Solutions:

1. **Busy Schedules:**

   o **Solution:** Schedule regular quality time, even if it's just 30 minutes a day.

2. **Stress or Burnout:**

   o **Solution:** Support each other by sharing responsibilities and finding ways to relax together.

3. **Complacency:**

   o **Solution:** Regularly reflect on what makes your partner special and look for ways to reignite the spark.

14.8 Practical Exercises for Sustaining Passion

Exercise 1: The Weekly Check-In

Set aside 30 minutes each week to talk about how you're feeling in the relationship. Share one thing you appreciated about each other and discuss any concerns constructively.

Exercise 2: Surprise Date Jar

Write down fun date ideas on slips of paper and place them in a jar. Take turns picking one out and doing it together.

Exercise 3: Gratitude Journals

Keep a journal where you each write something you're grateful for about the other person daily or weekly. Share your entries periodically.

Exercise 4: Create a Couples Bucket List

Sit down together and create a list of experiences or goals you want to achieve as a couple. Work toward checking them off together.

Conclusion

Sustaining passion and intimacy in a long-term relationship requires effort, but it's effort well worth making. By prioritizing emotional and physical connection, introducing novelty, and keeping communication strong, you can build a relationship that remains vibrant and exciting over time. Remember, passion isn't something that fades naturally—it's something that thrives when nurtured with care and intention.

In the next chapter, we'll explore how to become the best version of yourself so you can continue to grow as an individual while thriving in your relationship.

Chapter 15: Becoming the Best Version of Yourself: Confidence, Self-Love, and Mastery

A thriving relationship doesn't just depend on how much effort you put into your partner—it also depends on how much effort you put into yourself. The best relationships are built between two people who are confident, fulfilled, and constantly striving to grow as individuals.

This chapter focuses on becoming the best version of yourself, embracing self-love, and building confidence so you can bring your strongest, happiest self to the relationship. Whether you're dating, in a committed partnership, or married, your personal growth will positively impact every area of your life, including your romantic connection.

15.1 Why Self-Development Matters in Relationships

Your relationship with yourself sets the tone for every other relationship in your life. When you're confident, self-assured, and emotionally fulfilled, you naturally attract and maintain healthier, more balanced connections.

Benefits of Becoming Your Best Self:

- **Stronger Confidence:** You'll feel secure in your worth and bring that confidence into your relationship.

- **Better Boundaries:** Self-love allows you to set boundaries that protect your emotional well-being.

- **Increased Fulfillment:** Pursuing your passions and goals adds depth and excitement to your life, which benefits your relationship.

- **Reduced Insecurity:** When you're happy with yourself, you're less likely to seek validation or feel threatened by challenges.

15.2 Building Self-Love and Confidence

Self-love is the foundation of personal growth. It's about accepting yourself fully—flaws and all—and recognizing your inherent value.

How to Cultivate Self-Love:

1. **Practice Positive Self-Talk:** Replace negative thoughts like "I'm not good enough" with affirmations like "I am capable and deserving of love."

2. **Celebrate Your Achievements:** Acknowledge your successes, no matter how small.

3. **Forgive Yourself:** Let go of past mistakes and focus on learning and growing.

4. **Prioritize Self-Care:** Take care of your physical, emotional, and mental health through practices that nurture you.

How to Build Confidence:

- **Step Outside Your Comfort Zone:** Challenge yourself to try new things, even if they feel intimidating. Growth happens when you face your fears.

- **Focus on Strengths:** Identify what you're good at and lean into those abilities.

- **Set and Achieve Goals:** Accomplishing goals, no matter how small, reinforces your belief in your abilities.

15.3 Pursuing Personal Growth

Personal growth isn't just about self-improvement—it's about living a fulfilling life that inspires you and those around you.

Steps to Personal Growth:

1. **Set Clear Goals:** Identify what you want to achieve in different areas of your life, such as career, health, relationships, and hobbies.

2. **Embrace Lifelong Learning:** Read books, take courses, or learn new skills that challenge and excite you.

3. **Surround Yourself with Positive Influences:** Build a circle of friends and mentors who inspire and support your growth.

4. **Reflect Regularly:** Take time to reflect on your progress and adjust your path as needed.

15.4 Cultivating Emotional Resilience

Life and relationships come with challenges, but emotional resilience helps you navigate them with grace and strength.

How to Build Emotional Resilience:

- **Accept Change:** Embrace the idea that change is a natural part of life and relationships.

- **Practice Mindfulness:** Stay present in the moment and avoid dwelling on the past or worrying about the future.

- **Develop a Support System:** Lean on friends, family, or a therapist when you need encouragement.

- **Learn from Adversity:** View challenges as opportunities to grow and strengthen your character

15.5 Balancing Independence and Partnership

Maintaining your sense of self in a relationship is essential for long-term happiness. A healthy relationship allows both partners to grow individually while supporting each other.

How to Balance Independence and Connection:

- **Pursue Your Passions:** Continue exploring your interests and hobbies, even if they're separate from your partner's.

- **Respect Each Other's Space:** Give your partner the freedom to pursue their goals and interests as well.

- **Celebrate Each Other's Achievements:** Be genuinely happy for your partner's successes and encourage them to grow.

15.6 Embracing Self-Worth in Relationships

When you fully understand your worth, you're less likely to settle for less than you deserve. This mindset protects you from unhealthy dynamics and empowers you to seek relationships that align with your values.

Signs You're Embracing Your Worth:

- You set clear boundaries and stick to them.

- You prioritize your well-being and don't compromise your needs to please others.

- You walk away from relationships that don't align with your goals or values.

15.7 Staying Inspired and Motivated

The journey to becoming your best self is ongoing, and it's important to stay inspired along the way.

How to Stay Motivated:

- **Set New Challenges:** Always have something to work toward, whether it's a skill to learn, a fitness goal, or a creative project.

- **Celebrate Milestones:** Acknowledge and reward yourself for your progress.

- **Seek Inspiration:** Read books, listen to podcasts, or connect with people who inspire you to grow.

15.8 Practical Exercises for Self-Growth

Exercise 1: The Vision Board

Create a vision board that represents your goals and aspirations. Include images, quotes, and symbols that inspire you to grow and stay focused.

Exercise 2: Daily Affirmations

Write down three affirmations each morning that reinforce your confidence and self-worth. For example: "I am deserving of love and happiness."

Exercise 3: Monthly Reflection

At the end of each month, reflect on your progress. Ask yourself:

- What did I achieve this month?
- What challenges did I overcome?
- What can I improve next month?

Exercise 4: Self-Care Checklist

Create a checklist of self-care activities you enjoy, such as exercising, meditating, or spending time in nature. Commit to completing at least one activity each day.

Conclusion

Becoming the best version of yourself is a lifelong journey, but it's one of the most rewarding investments you can make. When you prioritize self-love, confidence, and personal growth, you not only enhance your life but also strengthen your relationships. Remember, the more fulfilled and inspired you are, the more you'll attract and maintain healthy, meaningful connections.

This book has given you the tools to approach, seduce, and build relationships with the men you desire—but the journey doesn't stop here. As you continue to grow and evolve, the possibilities for love, connection, and happiness are endless. Keep striving, keep shining, and never stop becoming the amazing person you're meant to be.

Bibliography

While this book is an original work based on a combination of research, observations, and insights into human behavior and relationships, several resources and concepts have informed the ideas presented. Below is a bibliography of books, studies, and theories that align with or have inspired the content in this book.

Books and Authors:

1. Allan, Barbara, and Allan Pease. *The Definitive Book of Body Language.* Bantam, 2006.
   o This book provided insights into nonverbal communication and how body language influences attraction.
2. Gottman, John, and Nan Silver. *The Seven Principles for Making Marriage Work.* Harmony, 1999.
   o The principles of emotional connection and communication discussed in this book align with the relationship-building techniques in this guide.
3. Gray, John. *Men Are from Mars, Women Are from Venus.* HarperCollins, 1992.
   o This classic text helped shape the understanding of gender communication dynamics.
4. Lerner, Harriet. *The Dance of Anger: A Woman's Guide to Changing the Patterns of Intimate Relationships.* Harper Perennial, 1985.
   o This book inspired the sections on emotional boundaries and conflict resolution.
5. Goulston, Mark. *Just Listen: Discover the Secret to Getting Through to Absolutely Anyone.* AMACOM, 2015.
   o The practical techniques for active listening in this book influenced the chapters on emotional connection and communication.

6. Fisher, Helen. *Why We Love: The Nature and Chemistry of Romantic Love.* Henry Holt and Co., 2004.
   - Fisher's research on the biology of love informed the understanding of attraction and chemistry in relationships.
7. Fine, Debra. *The Fine Art of Small Talk.* Hyperion, 2005.
   - This book contributed ideas on how to start and sustain engaging conversations.
8. Dyer, Wayne. *You'll See It When You Believe It.* HarperOne, 1989.
   - This work provided insights into self-love, confidence, and the law of attraction.
9. Tannen, Deborah. *You Just Don't Understand: Women and Men in Conversation.* Harper Perennial, 1990.
   - This book's exploration of conversational differences between men and women influenced the relationship communication strategies.
10. Perel, Esther. *Mating in Captivity: Unlocking Erotic Intelligence.* Harper, 2006.
    - Perel's work on sustaining passion and intimacy in long-term relationships inspired several chapters in this book.

Scientific Studies and Articles:

1. Mehrabian, Albert. "Communication Without Words." *Psychology Today,* 1967.
   - This foundational study on nonverbal communication shaped the chapter on body language.
2. Fisher, Helen E., et al. "Romantic Love: A Mammalian Brain System for Mate Choice." *Philosophical Transactions of the Royal Society B: Biological Sciences,* 2006.
   - The understanding of the brain's role in attraction and desire drew on Fisher's research.

3. Baumeister, Roy F., and Mark R. Leary. "The Need to Belong: Desire for Interpersonal Attachments as a Fundamental Human Motivation." *Psychological Bulletin,* 1995.
   o This study informed sections on emotional bonding and the importance of connection.
4. Aron, Arthur, et al. "The Experimental Generation of Interpersonal Closeness: A Procedure and Some Preliminary Findings." *Personality and Social Psychology Bulletin,* 1997.
   o This study on building intimacy through personal questions influenced the chapter on emotional connection.

Theories and Frameworks Referenced:

- **Attachment Theory:** John Bowlby's and Mary Ainsworth's work on attachment styles helped shape the understanding of emotional needs and dynamics in relationships.
- **The Triangular Theory of Love:** Psychologist Robert Sternberg's theory on the components of love (intimacy, passion, and commitment) informed sections on building and maintaining romantic relationships.
- **The Five Love Languages:** Gary Chapman's framework on understanding how people express and receive love shaped the discussions on emotional intimacy and connection.

This bibliography acknowledges the broader field of research and expertise that has informed the ideas explored in this book. While much of the content is based on practical insights and advice, these resources provided inspiration and a foundation for key concepts.

Glossary

This glossary provides definitions and explanations of key terms and concepts used throughout *The Last Book You'll Ever Need to Read to Approach, Seduce, and Bed the Men You Desire: Mastering the Art of Attraction for Dating, Relationships, and Marriage.*

Active Listening: A communication technique in which the listener fully focuses on, understands, and responds thoughtfully to the speaker. It involves making eye contact, nodding, and providing verbal feedback to show engagement.

Attraction: The emotional, physical, or psychological pull toward someone, often rooted in factors like chemistry, shared interests, and physical appeal.

Attachment Styles: Patterns of emotional bonding and behavior in relationships, often categorized as secure, anxious, avoidant, or disorganized. These styles influence how people connect and respond to intimacy.

Body Language: Nonverbal communication expressed through posture, gestures, facial expressions, and movement. Body language often conveys emotions and intentions more strongly than words.

Boundaries: Personal limits set to define what is acceptable behavior from others. Healthy boundaries protect emotional well-being and promote mutual respect in relationships.

Chemistry: The emotional and physical connection between two people, often described as a spark or intense attraction.

Commitment: The decision to invest in a relationship and prioritize it over other romantic or casual connections. Commitment often involves exclusivity, trust, and shared goals.

Communication: The process of sharing thoughts, feelings, and information through verbal and nonverbal means. Effective communication is essential for building emotional intimacy and resolving conflicts.

Confidence: A belief in one's abilities, worth, and attractiveness. Confidence is a key component of magnetism and plays a significant role in how others perceive you.

Emotional Intimacy: A deep sense of closeness and connection in which both partners feel understood, valued, and safe to express their feelings and vulnerabilities.

Emotional Safety: The feeling of being accepted and supported without fear of judgment or rejection. Emotional safety allows for honest communication and vulnerability in a relationship.

Flirting: A playful and often subtle way of expressing romantic or sexual interest through words, gestures, or body language.

Friend Zone: A relationship dynamic in which one person sees the other only as a friend, while the other desires a romantic connection.

Gaslighting: A form of emotional manipulation in which someone causes another person to doubt their perceptions, feelings, or reality. This behavior is often a red flag in relationships.

Intimacy: The closeness and connection shared between two people, encompassing emotional, physical, and intellectual bonding.

Love Languages: A concept developed by Gary Chapman, describing five primary ways people express and receive love: words of affirmation, acts of service, receiving gifts, quality time, and physical touch.

Magnetic Chemistry: The dynamic energy between two people that creates intense attraction and intrigue, often driven by a mix of physical, emotional, and psychological factors.

Mystery: The element of intrigue created by keeping some aspects of yourself undisclosed, encouraging curiosity and interest. Mystery helps maintain excitement in relationships.

Red Flags: Warning signs that indicate potential problems in a relationship, such as dishonesty, inconsistency, or lack of respect. Recognizing red flags helps protect emotional well-being.

Seduction: The process of creating desire and attraction, often by using charm, body language, and emotional connection to captivate someone's interest.

Self-Love: The practice of appreciating and nurturing yourself by recognizing your worth, setting boundaries, and prioritizing your well-being.

Sexual Tension: The charged energy and anticipation between two people who are attracted to each other, often created through subtle cues like body language and tone of voice.

Trust: The belief in someone's reliability, honesty, and intentions. Trust is a fundamental component of healthy relationships.

Vulnerability: The willingness to share your feelings, fears, and experiences openly, even at the risk of rejection. Vulnerability fosters deeper emotional intimacy and trust.

This glossary provides clarity on the concepts and terminology central to building attraction, emotional connection, and fulfilling relationships. Let me know if you'd like to expand or customize it further!

www.ingramcontent.com/pod-product-compliance
Lightning Source LLC
Chambersburg PA
CBHW071559040426
42452CB00008B/1226